Entertaining with

BLUEGRASS WINNERS

COOKBOOK

NEW RECIPES AND MENUS FROM KENTUCKY'S LEGENDARY HORSE FARMS

Farm histories by Edward L. Bowen

Garden Club of Lexington, Inc.

Lexington, Kentucky

Member of the Garden Club of America

Library of Congress Control Number: 2007904787

ISBN: 978-1-58150--174-2
Printed in China
First Edition: 2008

Proceeds from the sale of *Entertaining with Bluegrass Winners Cookbook*
benefit the community through projects of the Garden Club of Lexington, Inc.
P.O. Box 22091, Lexington, Kentucky 40522
(859) 255-8095

a division of
Blood-Horse Publications
PUBLISHERS SINCE 1916

TABLE OF CONTENTS

CONTENTS

FALL

CONTENTS

INTRODUCTION

The ladies of the Garden Club of Lexington have undertaken the bold task of creating a second cookbook, one that reflects the intimate relationship among horse farms, entertaining, and seasonal menus.

It is typical for festive meals and parties to be the likely settings when Thoroughbred industry people strike deals, exchange information, or celebrate successes. *Entertaining with Bluegrass Winners* is a new compilation of menus and recipes that provide a fresh way to entertain, whether it's a family gathering, a post-sale buffet, or a lavish party.

The initial cookbook, *Bluegrass Winners*, was a favorite, selling 100,000 copies in seven printings and garnering much praise for its savory recipes and beautiful photos that provide a glimpse into the Bluegrass style of entertaining.

More than 20 years later, *Entertaining with Bluegrass Winners* continues that tradition with updated recipes and menus and with the same delicious outcomes and photos that allow readers to see behind the gates of area horse farms. Indeed, the new book honors the spirit of the original contributors, many of whose daughters are responsible for the recipes that follow.

Kentucky is blessed with four distinct seasons that bring beauty to the garden as well as to the table. Favorite Southern recipes are placed side by side with innovative creations that use the freshest ingredients, keeping the changing seasons in mind.

As with the sales of the first cookbook, the proceeds from *Entertaining with Bluegrass Winners* support the gardens at Ashland, the Henry Clay Estate. Clay was one of the early horsemen and purveyors of hospitality in Lexington. His political savvy also led to his being called the Great Compromiser and Sage of the West. He entertained the foremost statesmen of his time at his six-hundred-acre home, where he raised fine Thoroughbreds.

In 1950, after the Henry Clay Foundation had become a reality and Ashland opened to the public, the garden club was asked to create a garden on the grounds. Henry F. Kenney of Cincinnati was chosen to draw a plan for the garden as well as a plan for the overall planting of the 20 acres. The Garden Club of Lexington undertook the endeavor of planting and maintaining the garden, a tradition that continues today.

When the garden began to outstrip the resources of the garden club, members came up with the idea of publishing a cookbook with a horse farm theme. It proved to be a big success. The garden club hopes to continue this tradition with *Entertaining with Bluegrass Winners* — a tribute to the Bluegrass style of entertaining and the bounty of the land.

SPRING

AIRDRIE STUD

SPRING LUNCHEON

Cream of Watercress Soup with Melba Toast

Kentucky Bibb Lettuce with Strawberries and Feta Cheese

Stir-Fried Asparagus with Sesame Seeds

Poached Salmon with Caper and Dill Sauce

Lemon Pudding

Former Kentucky Governor Brereton C. Jones and his wife, Libby, have nurtured and built upon the history of a property that served as a cornerstone for the Thoroughbred breeding industry. The heart of their Airdrie Farm, along historic Old Frankfort Pike, occupies part of a 5,000-acre land grant acquired by Mrs. Jones' ancestor Robert Alexander in 1790. The property, named Woodburn, rose to fame under Alexander's son, R.A. Alexander. Woodburn was home to Lexington, who reigned as America's greatest sire for sixteen years, a period that included the Civil War. Woodburn set a precedent in the emerging Kentucky breeding scene by producing horses largely for the commercial market rather than its private racing stable. This early practice gave rise to the concentration of expertise in horse husbandry as well as the collection of top-quality breeding stock that has endured in Kentucky through the years.

Governor and Mrs. Jones operated a portion of Woodburn as Airdrie Stud for many years before expanding their property to include the old Woodburn house with its stately columns and handsomely appointed rooms that have been restored to their former splendor. Mrs. Jones also revived the gardens designed by Jens Jensen of Denmark, dating from 1916.

The breeding and sales operation and highly successful stallion roster continue under Airdrie's name. While Airdrie's past is praiseworthy, its future is equally exciting with young stallions that are rapidly rising to the top of national statistics. Since 1972 Airdrie Stud has produced more than one hundred fifty stakes winners and the earners of more than $100 million on the racetrack.

CREAM OF WATERCRESS SOUP

3 leeks, white part only, chopped

1 medium-sized onion, chopped

3 to 5 tablespoons butter

3 Idaho potatoes, peeled & chopped

3 cups chicken stock

3 teaspoons kosher salt

Cayenne pepper to taste

2 bunches of watercress

1 quart half & half

Sprigs of watercress or fresh parsley for garnish

Salt and pepper to taste

- Sauté leeks and onion in butter; do not let brown. Add potatoes, stock, salt, and cayenne pepper. Cover and cook slowly until vegetables are soft.

- Allow mixture to cool slightly and blend in blender or food processor in batches until smooth.

- Blanch watercress in boiling water 2 minutes (to keep the acid from curdling the soup). Drain and purée in blender or food processor.

- Combine all ingredients in clean soup pot and slowly add half & half. If soup is too thick, add some milk to achieve desired consistency.

- Season to taste. This soup is better if made a day ahead.

- Serve hot or cold. Garnish with reserved watercress sprigs or fresh parsley.

SERVES 8 TO 10

MELBA TOAST

1 loaf Pepperidge Farm Very Thin White Bread

2 cups butter, melted

- Preheat oven to 275°F.

- Cut bread slices in half diagonally. Place in a single layer on cookie sheets. Bake in preheated oven for 20 minutes.

- Using tongs, dip each slice in melted butter and tap off excess.

- Return to cookie sheet. Bake 20 to 25 minutes more or until golden-brown.

- Cool on brown paper grocery bag, opened flat. Store in an airtight container.

MAKES APPROXIMATELY 4 DOZEN PIECES

KENTUCKY BIBB LETTUCE WITH STRAWBERRIES AND FETA CHEESE

SALAD

5 to 6 heads Bibb or Boston
lettuce, washed and dried

1 quart strawberries, sliced
(small strawberries are best)

1 pound feta cheese

¾ cup almonds, sliced (optional)

DRESSING

¾ cup sugar

1 cup cider vinegar

1 teaspoon dry mustard

¾ cup vegetable oil

1 teaspoon salt

1 teaspoon paprika

2–3 cloves garlic, minced

(Can be made several days ahead)

- To make dressing, heat sugar and vinegar until sugar has dissolved. Remove from heat.

- Add mustard, oil, salt, paprika, garlic, and almonds (if used). Mix well.

- To prepare salad, toss cleaned lettuce with dressing and arrange on plates.

- Place strawberries and feta cheese and almonds on top of lettuce. Serve immediately.

SERVES 8 TO 10

STIR-FRIED ASPARAGUS WITH SESAME SEEDS

4 teaspoons sesame oil

3 teaspoons minced fresh ginger

24 asparagus stalks, washed
and peeled

½ cup red bell pepper, julienned

½ cup scallions, julienned

½ cup toasted pine nuts

1½ teaspoons toasted white
sesame seeds

Salt and pepper to taste

- Pour sesame oil in a wok or sauté pan and heat until the oil is very hot. Add the ginger and stir for a few seconds.

- Add asparagus and stir-fry for a couple minutes, until cooked but still firm and bright in color.

- Add bell pepper and scallions and cook for 1 minute. Add pine nuts and sesame seeds and heat through. Season with salt and pepper to taste and serve immediately.

SERVES 6 TO 8

POACHED SALMON

2–3 lemons, sliced in rounds

1–2 bay leaves

1 scant tablespoon peppercorns

Equal parts of white wine and
water (enough just to cover
the fish)

4–5 pounds salmon

- Slice lemons thin; line bottom of poacher or roasting pan
  with lemon slices.

- Add bay leaves, peppercorns, white wine, and water.
  Cover this mixture with aluminum foil. Boil for one minute.

- Place salmon in poacher, skin side down. Adjust liquids to ensure
  fish is covered.

- Place foil over poacher again and cook 4 to 5 minutes (white will
  show between the meat of the fish).

- Turn off heat and allow pan to sit till slightly cooled.

- Remove salmon from pan. The skin should peel off easily
  at this point.

- Cover and chill until ready to serve with caper and dill sauce
  (recipe below).

SERVES 8 TO 10

CAPER AND DILL SAUCE

1 cup mayonnaise

¼ cup lemon juice

½ small (3-ounce) jar of capers,
drained

⅛ cup onion minced

2 teaspoons fresh dill chopped

- Mix above ingredients well, chill, and serve
  with poached salmon.

- Can be made a day ahead and kept refrigerated.

LEMON PUDDING

2 cups sugar

6 tablespoons flour

2 cups milk

4 eggs, separated

½ teaspoon salt

2 teaspoons grated lemon zest

Juice of 2 lemons

- Preheat oven to 350°F. Butter a 6-cup soufflé dish.

- In large bowl, combine sugar and flour; then add milk, well-beaten egg yolks, salt, lemon juice, and lemon zest.

- With electric mixer, beat egg whites until stiff. Carefully fold egg whites into sugar and flour mixture. Do not over mix as this will flatten egg whites.

- Pour mixture into soufflé dish. Set dish in pan of warm water.

- Bake for 35 to 40 minutes, or until knife inserted comes out clean. When done, this pudding forms a light fluffy cake on top and a rich sauce on bottom.

SERVES 10

ASHLAND GARDENS

TEA IN THE GARDEN

Olive-Nut Sandwiches

Kentucky Country Ham Spread

Crab Salad in Cucumber Boats

Watercress Sandwiches

Benedictine Finger Sandwiches

Zucchini Soup

Apricot Jam Bars

The "Best" Iced Sugar Cookies

Grand Marnier Icing

The formal garden at Ashland, the Henry Clay Estate, dates from 1950 when the Garden Club of Lexington Inc. was asked by the Henry Clay Foundation to undertake its creation. The club chose landscape architect Henry Fletcher Kenney of Cincinnati to draw up a ten-year plan and design for the garden. Work began in 1951, with different sections of the formal eighteenth-century-style garden reaching completion in the ensuing years. A dipping pool, birdbath, benches, and a hundred-year-old bronze figure of a child by Raingo were added later. Today the garden is composed of six parterres, including a rose garden and an herb garden, all surrounded by perennial borders.

In 1986 a Saunders hybrid peony garden was planted just east of the formal walled garden, the flowers given by Mrs. Richard Prewitt in memory of her daughter. The many varieties of peonies create a breathtaking display in early summer.

Garden Club members did most of the work in executing the original plan, and members still meet each Wednesday of the growing season to plan, plant, and tend the beds. Throughout the year, many Ashland visitors discover the gardens, finding a quiet place where they can walk, rest, meet friends — or just enjoy the tranquil surroundings.

OLIVE-NUT SANDWICHES

2 8-ounce packages cream cheese, softened

1 cup mayonnaise

4 tablespoons olive juice

Dash of black pepper

1 cup chopped pecans

2 cups chopped salad olives

2 loaves of very thin-sliced bread (a mixture of white and whole wheat is more colorful)

Parsley sprigs or olive slices for garnish

- Combine all ingredients for spread and mix well.

- Cover and refrigerate for at least 4 hours so mixture will thicken.

- Spread on very thin bread, top with another slice of bread, remove crusts, and cut into 4 triangles. Garnish with parsley sprig or a sliver of olive.

- Mixture will last three weeks in refrigerator.

SERVES 16 (YIELDS 58 TRIANGULAR SANDWICHES)

KENTUCKY COUNTRY HAM SPREAD

¾ pound Kentucky country ham, finely ground

4 ounces cream cheese, softened

Worcestershire sauce to taste

Freshly ground black pepper to taste

3 heaping tablespoons mayonnaise

4 tablespoons fresh flat-leaf parsley, chopped

Juice of 1 lemon

Extra flat-leaf parsley for garnish

- Combine all ingredients with mixer, blender, or food processor (on pulse speed).

- Correct seasoning to taste and form mixture into oblong shape on serving platter, and sprinkle with additional parsley for color.

- Cover and refrigerate for up to 2 days.

- Serve with toast points or bland crackers.

SERVES 16

CRAB SALAD IN CUCUMBER BOATS

1 pound crab meat, picked over to remove shell pieces

1 teaspoon capers

⅓ cup mayonnaise

1 tablespoon minced onion

1–2 teaspoons fresh lemon juice

Salt and pepper to taste

¼ cup finely chopped celery

A dash of Worcestershire and Tabasco sauces

4 medium cucumbers

Paprika for garnish

- Combine all ingredients, except the cucumber.

- Peel cucumber completely or, if you prefer, in stripes to leave some green peel for color.

- Cut cucumber in half crosswise. Carefully remove seeds with melon-ball spoon.

- Stuff cucumbers with crab mixture, cover, and refrigerate for 1 hour.

- Slice cucumber halves into ½-inch rounds and sprinkle with paprika.

- These can be covered and refrigerated for a few hours before serving.

SERVES 16

WATERCRESS SANDWICHES

3 ounces cream cheese, softened

1 tablespoon fresh lemon juice

½ cup sour cream

1 teaspoon finely chopped chives

Dash of Worcestershire sauce

Salt to taste

1 cup fresh watercress, chopped & lightly packed

18 thinly sliced white bread slices, crusts removed

2 tablespoons butter, softened

- Blend cream cheese, lemon juice, sour cream, chives, and seasoning.
- Stir in watercress.
- Flatten each slice of bread with rolling pin.
- Spread bread lightly with butter and then watercress mixture.
- Roll each piece in jelly-roll fashion and arrange side by side in shallow pan.
- Cover bread with damp cloth and refrigerate for at least 1 hour.
- To serve, cut each roll in half, so each half is about 1½ inches long. Garnish with a watercress sprig.
- These can be made a day ahead.

SERVES 16 OR MAKES 36 SMALL SANDWICHES

BENEDICTINE FINGER SANDWICHES

1½ large cucumbers, seeded and chopped

16 ounces cream cheese, softened

2 scallions, white part only, finely chopped

A drop of green food coloring

2–3 tablespoons mayonnaise

6–7 slices bacon, crisply cooked and crumbled

Salt and pepper to taste

2 loaves of very thin white or wheat bread

- Using a paper towel, squeeze most of moisture from cucumber pieces.
- Combine cream cheese, cucumbers, onions, food coloring, and mayonnaise with electric mixer.
- Add bacon and salt and pepper to taste.
- Prepare slices of very thin white or wheat bread by removing crusts.
- Spread Benedictine mixture on bread. Cover with second slice and cut diagonally to make two triangular sandwiches.
- Store sandwiches, covered with damp paper towel, in airtight container in refrigerator until ready to serve.

MAKES APPROXIMATELY 24 SANDWICHES

ZUCCHINI SOUP

2 tablespoons butter

2 tablespoons onions, chopped

1 clove garlic, chopped

1 pound zucchini, sliced

½ teaspoon curry powder

1 teaspoon salt

1⅓ cups chicken broth

½ cup heavy cream

Sour cream and chopped chives
　for garnish

- Heat butter in pan over medium heat. Sauté onions, garlic, and zucchini in butter for about 10 minutes or until soft.

- Remove from heat and cool slightly. Place onions, garlic, and zucchini in blender or food processor along with curry powder, salt, and broth, and pulse two or three times. Carefully add cream, stirring carefully until well blended.

- Season to taste. Refrigerate to serve cold or heat slowly on stove to serve warm. Garnish with dollop of sour cream and chopped chives.

SERVES 6

APRICOT JAM BARS

1 cup all-purpose (plain) flour

1 cup confectioner's sugar

1¼ cups sliced almonds or equal
　amount of quick oats

1 stick unsalted butter

6 ounces seedless apricot jam
　(or other flavor of your choice)

- Preheat oven to 375°F.

- Combine flour, confectioner's sugar, 1 cup sliced almonds (or oats), and butter in food processor until mixture is fine and crumbly.

- Press ⅔ of the mixture into greased 9x9-inch baking pan to form crust.

- Evenly spread apricot jam (or flavor of your choice) on crust.

- Top with remaining crumb mixture and ¼ cup sliced almonds (or oats).

- Bake for 18–20 minutes or until golden-brown. Allow to cool; then cut into bars and serve.

SERVES 16

THE "BEST" ICED SUGAR COOKIES

¼ cup unsalted butter,
   at room temperature

¾ cup sugar

½ teaspoon vanilla extract

1 tablespoon grated orange zest

1 egg

4 teaspoons milk

2 cups flour

1½ teaspoons baking powder

¼ teaspoon salt

- Cream butter and sugar together.

- Add vanilla, orange zest, egg, and milk.

- In separate bowl, sift together flour, baking powder, and salt. Add to creamed mixture to make stiff dough.

- Refrigerate for 1 hour or so.

- Roll out dough on floured surface to ¼-inch thickness.

- Cut into desired shapes with cookie cutters.

- Bake at 325°F until golden.

SERVES 16

GRAND MARNIER ICING

¼ cup unsalted butter,
   at room temperature

1 pound (3½ cups) sifted
   confectioner's sugar

¼ teaspoon salt

1 tablespoon vanilla extract

1 tablespoon lemon extract

1–2 tablespoons Grand Marnier
   liqueur

4–5 tablespoons heavy cream

A tiny dot of desired food
   coloring (we suggest pink)

- Cream butter. Add about one cup of sugar and all of the salt. Cream well.

- Add vanilla, lemon extract, and Grand Marnier.

- Add remaining sugar, alternating with cream, using enough cream to give icing a slight gloss and good spreading consistency. If using food coloring, add one or two drops at this time.

- Ice the cookies.

SERVES 16

COBRA FARM

DERBY COCKTAILS

Baby Browns

Crab Salad

Steamed Kentucky Beans with Cucumber Dipping Sauce

Bourbon Pork Tenderloin with Rolls

Mushroom Canapés

Corn Fritters

Golden Bars

Cobra Farm has a successful pattern of being named in honor of its owner's other ventures. Cobra was the name of the golf club company that owner Gary Biszantz built, nurtured, and finally sold so he could pursue another passion, Thoroughbred racing. Back in 1974 the core of the farm was named for the White Horse Tavern of owner Ben Castleman. It was on White Horse Acres that Castleman bred 1977 Triple Crown winner Seattle Slew. Coincidentally, that remarkable champion was to figure in one of the key successes of the current Cobra Farm, for he was the grandsire of the brilliant Old Trieste, who carried Biszantz' colors to several important victories.

Biszantz bought his first racehorse in 1956 while in his early twenties, but racing was only a sideline then. After success with his father's and then his own automobile dealership, Biszantz moved into the head office of Cobra Golf, which he co-owned, originally, as another sideline. He had been Athlete of the Year at Claremont College and later won numerous California golf tournaments. The golf equipment sideline burgeoned under his leadership, and when sold to American Brands, in 1996, it was the second-largest manufacturer of oversized golf clubs.

By then Biszantz had purchased eighty-two acres of the former White Horse operation, and he renamed it Cobra Farm. Later purchases raised the property to 340 acres, now home to a select broodmare band and its produce. Biszantz accepted the challenges of leadership in his beloved sport and served several years as chairman of the Thoroughbred Owners and Breeders Association.

BABY BROWNS

1 loaf (24 slices) very thin sliced
   white bread

6 tablespoons unsalted butter,
   melted

¾ teaspoon chicken base

¼ cup hot water

¾ cup whole milk

3 tablespoons unsalted butter

2 tablespoons all-purpose flour

½ teaspoon Worcestershire sauce

½ cup grated cheddar cheese

¼ cup finely grated
   Parmesan cheese

6 ounces thinly sliced turkey

8 cherry tomatoes, chopped

6 pieces bacon, cooked
   and crumbled

- Use a 2¾-inch round cookie cutter or glass rim to cut circles from 24 slices of bread. Flatten bread rounds with rolling pin.

- Spray the cups of 2 miniature muffin tins with cooking oil.

- Brush top side of each bread round with melted butter and gently press into miniature muffin tin cup. Moisten finger with butter to press folds of bread against sides and to seal any splits.

- Bake bread cups in 350°F oven for 10 minutes.

- Dissolve chicken base in water and add milk.

- Melt 3 tablespoons butter in sauce pan and add flour, stirring with whisk until blended.

- Blend in chicken base mixture and stir until thickened.

- Add Worcestershire sauce and cheeses and stir until smooth.

- Chop sliced turkey into small pieces and place a little in bottom of each cup.

- Add chopped tomatoes, cheese sauce, and top with bacon crumbles.

- Bake at 350°F for 10 minutes.

MAKES 24 APPETIZER VERSIONS OF KENTUCKY HOT BROWN SANDWICHES

CRAB SALAD

2 cups white onions, thinly sliced

2½ pounds crab meat

6–7 bay leaves

1 cup cider vinegar

1 cup salad oil

1 teaspoon salt

2 teaspoons celery seed

2 tablespoons capers

Dash of Tabasco sauce

- In large serving bowl, spread half of onions over bottom of bowl. Cover onions with cleaned crab meat. Top with remaining onion.

- In large glass jar, mix remaining ingredients and shake well.

- Pour marinade over crab and onion mixture. Cover and chill for 2 to 12 hours.

- Toss lightly before serving with crackers or toast cups (use mini phyllo shells found in frozen foods section of grocery).

SERVES 10 TO 12

STEAMED KENTUCKY BEANS

1½ pounds fresh Kentucky
    green beans

Salt

Water

- Clean and cut tips off of beans.

- Place beans in large heatproof glass bowl. Add salt to enough water to cover bottom of dish, just slightly covering some of beans (you essentially "steam" beans). Cover bowl with plastic wrap and microwave 2 to 3 minutes.

- Remove from microwave, drain water, and place beans in ice bath. Allow beans to cool and pat dry.

- Serve with cucumber dip. (Beans can be made day ahead and stored in refrigerator until ready to use.)

SERVES 12

CUCUMBER DIPPING SAUCE

1 large cucumber, peeled,
    seeded, and grated on large hole
    of box grater

1 tablespoon chopped shallots

¾ cup sour cream

¼ cup buttermilk

¼ cup mayonnaise

3 tablespoons lemon juice

1½ teaspoons kosher salt

Pinch of cayenne pepper

4 tablespoons finely chopped flat-
    leaf parsley

3 tablespoons chopped fresh chives

- Mix all ingredients in medium bowl. Adjust seasoning with salt and cayenne.

- This sauce is better made 1 day ahead.

- Serve with green beans or any other crisp vegetables.

BOURBON PORK TENDERLOIN WITH ROLLS

2 large pork tenderloins

2 dozen rolls for sliced tenderloin

MARINADE

¾ cup bourbon

3 tablespoons brown sugar

¼ cup water

1 teaspoon kosher salt

½ cup soy sauce

½ teaspoon ginger

⅓ cup canola oil

1 teaspoon white pepper

¼ cup Worcestershire sauce

2 tablespoons freshly ground
    black pepper

5 cloves garlic, diced

- Mix marinade ingredients together. Pour marinade into large resealable plastic bag and add tenderloins. Marinate for at least 4 hours or overnight.

- Heat grill, remove tenderloins from plastic bag, and cook on grill until done.

- Slice thin and serve with small rolls and mustard.

SERVES 12

MUSHROOM CANAPÉS

24 slices Pepperidge Farm
    Party Rye

4 tablespoons butter

½ pound fresh mushrooms,
    coarsely chopped

1 teaspoon grated shallots

2 tablespoons chopped
    flat-leaf parsley

½ cup sour cream

Paprika for garnish

- Preheat oven to 350°F.

- With 1½-inch biscuit cutter, cut 1 small circle from each bread slice; place bread rounds on baking sheet. Toast on 1 side for 3 minutes. Remove rounds from oven and turn toasted side down on baking sheet.

- Heat butter in saucepan and sauté mushrooms and shallots until browned. Remove from heat.

- Combine parsley with sour cream; add to mushrooms.

- Put a mound of mixture on untoasted side of bread. Dust with paprika.

- Bake in oven for 15 minutes or until browned. Serve immediately.

MAKES 2 DOZEN

CORN FRITTERS

2 eggs

1 cup milk

2 cups fresh cut corn or canned corn, drained

1 tablespoon sugar

1½ teaspoons salt

2 teaspoons baking powder

½ teaspoon paprika

2 tablespoons shortening, melted

- Beat eggs and milk, add remaining ingredients, and mix thoroughly.

- Drop by spoonfuls into deep hot oil (365°F) until fritters turn golden-brown. Use enough oil to cover fritters when dropped into the oil.

- Drain on paper towels. Serve immediately.

MAKES APPROXIMATELY 24 TO 30 FRITTERS

GOLDEN BARS

1½ cups firmly packed brown sugar

½ cup unsalted butter, softened

1 cup quick-cooking rolled oats (uncooked)

1 egg

¾ cup all-purpose flour

1 tablespoon lemon juice

½ teaspoon salt

1 teaspoon vanilla

¼ teaspoon baking soda

½ cup chopped walnuts or pecans

- Preheat oven to 350°F.

- Combine all ingredients except nuts in large mixing bowl.

- Mix at low speed until well blended.

- Stir in nuts.

- Pour into greased 8-inch square baking pan.

- Bake at 350°F for 40 to 45 minutes.

- Allow to cool and cut into 24 bars.

MAKES APPROXIMATELY 24 BARS

DARLEY STUD

AFTER A STALLION SHOWING

Fried Oysters with Chili Sauce

Stone Crab Claws with Three Sauces

Leek and Prosciutto Tart

Loaded Roasted Fingerling Potatoes

Lamb Cutlets with Apricot Horseradish Sauce

Almond Cookies

Chocolate Drop Cookies

Sheikh Mohammed bin Rashid al Maktoum, ruler of Dubai, purchased Jonabell Farm, known for its stone water tower, from the family of John A. Bell III in 2001. Bell had purchased the core of the farm in 1954, developing it into a successful breeding operation and birthplace of such champions as Damascus and Epitome.

Darley covers some eight hundred acres and is headquarters for Sheikh Mohammed's U.S. stallion operation. The stallion roster has included four sires of recent Kentucky Derby winners: Street Cry (sire of Street Sense, 2007), Holy Bull (Giacomo, 2005), Elusive Quality (Smarty Jones, 2004), and Quiet American (Real Quiet, 1998). Preakness winner Bernardini is among stallions at Darley, and Street Sense was to join the roster upon his retirement from racing. A memorial statue of the late Triple Crown winner Affirmed marks his grave near the stallion barns.

Sheikh Mohammed has several other properties in the surrounding area: Raceland Farm in Paris, which serves as a yearling division; Gainsborough Farm, which he inherited from his late brother Sheikh Maktoum in 2006 and which serves as a broodmare division; and the newest Kentucky Darley division on James Lane. Collectively his properties total nearly four thousand acres in the Central Kentucky area.

With the focus of being a leader in the Thoroughbred world, Darley also has farms in England, Ireland, Japan, Australia, and Dubai. Each operation strives to preserve the history of the land, the sport, and the breed while looking to the future of this industry.

FRIED OYSTERS

8 pints large oysters, drained

2 boxes saltine crackers,
 finely crushed

Vegetable or canola oil

Salt and fresh ground
 black pepper to taste

- Heat oil in deep fryer or deep pan on stove, reaching 350°F but reducing heat to 325°F before cooking oysters.

- Spread cracker crumbs on cookie sheet. Drain oysters; then roll in cracker crumbs. Roll oysters two more times with a rest time of 1 to 5 minutes between each coating.

- Place oysters in fryer basket without crowding them (this ensures even cooking). Lower slowly into oil and cook until golden brown, approximately 5 minutes.

- Drain oysters on cookie sheet with paper towels. Season with salt and pepper.

- Serve immediately with seafood chili sauce (recipe below).

SERVES 24 AS APPETIZER

CHILI SAUCE

1 cup chili sauce

1 cup ketchup

5 tablespoons prepared horseradish

4 teaspoons freshly squeezed
 lemon juice

1 teaspoon Worcestershire sauce

½ teaspoon Tabasco sauce

- Combine all ingredients and serve with seafood. This can be made several days ahead and refrigerated until ready to use.

MAKES 3 CUPS

STONE CRAB CLAWS WITH THREE SAUCES

CHIPOTLE AIOLI

6 egg yolks

6 whole eggs

9 cloves garlic

9 tablespoons lemon juice

3 tablespoons adobo sauce (sauce from chipotles)

9 tablespoons chopped chipotle chiles (no seeds)

6 teaspoons salt

12 cups blended oil

MUSTARD SAUCE

1 quart mayonnaise

¼ (6-ounce) bottle steak sauce

½ (5-ounce) jar Dijon mustard

1 tablespoon dry mustard

2½ tablespoons Worcestershire sauce

Dash of Tabasco sauce

1 tablespoon tarragon (optional)

HORSERADISH SAUCE

2 cups sour cream

1½ cups mayonnaise

2 teaspoons lemon juice

8 teaspoons drained, prepared horseradish

Salt to taste

White pepper to taste

- Buy prepared claws. Crack and serve with chipotle aioli, mustard, and horseradish sauces.

Chipotle Aioli:

- Combine all ingredients except oil in food processor or blender. Begin processing and slowly add oil. Should achieve mayonnaise consistency.

Mustard Sauce:

- Combine ingredients in large bowl; stir to mix; then use electric mixer to blend well.

Horseradish Sauce:

- Blend all ingredients and chill for 3 to 4 hours.

SERVES 12 TO 14

LEEK AND PROSCIUTTO TART

All-purpose flour for dusting

½ pound frozen, prepared puff pastry, thawed

2 tablespoons extra virgin olive oil

1½ cups (about 3 medium) leeks, well washed, halved lengthwise, and thinly sliced. White and tender greens only.

2 teaspoons fresh thyme, finely chopped

Salt and pepper to taste

2 cups Gruyere cheese, coarsely shredded

3–4 thinly sliced pieces of prosciutto, cut into strips

1 tablespoon melted unsalted butter

- Spray large baking sheet with nonstick spray and preheat oven to 425°F.

- On lightly floured surface, roll out puff pastry into 13-inch square, fold corners in, and gently roll pastry into rough round.

- Transfer to baking sheet and cover with damp tea towel. Refrigerate. In large skillet, heat olive oil; sauté leeks and thyme. Salt and pepper to taste. Cook until soft, 5 minutes.

- Remove baking sheet with tart shell from the refrigerator, sprinkle half of cheese over pastry leaving 1-inch border; then cover with leeks, prosciutto, and remaining cheese.

- Fold tart edges to form rim. Brush pastry edges with melted butter for color.

- Bake 20 minutes or until golden. Blot excess oil from edges with paper towel.

- Cool slightly before cutting into wedges.

- This can be prepared ahead and served at room temperature.

SERVES 10 PEOPLE

LOADED ROASTED FINGERLING POTATOES

4 pounds unpeeled small fingerling potatoes, halved lengthwise

3 tablespoons olive oil

2 teaspoons finely chopped fresh rosemary

Salt and pepper to taste

1½ cups chilled sour cream

2 ounces black caviar (about ¼ cup)

- Preheat oven to 400°F.

- Combine potatoes, 2 tablespoons olive oil, and rosemary in large bowl. Season with salt and pepper and toss to coat.

- Prepare large, rimmed baking sheet with 1 tablespoon oil. Arrange potatoes, cut side down, in single layer. Shake pan so as to prevent sticking.

- Roast until potatoes are brown, crisp, and cooked through, about 35 minutes.

- After cooling potatoes for about 10 minutes, put dollop of sour cream and a sprinkling of caviar on each potato and serve.

SERVES 12

LAMB CUTLETS

3 racks of lamb (approximately 6 bones each)

3 tablespoons olive oil

2½ tablespoons fresh rosemary

8 garlic cloves, minced

2 teaspoons salt

2 teaspoons freshly ground black pepper

- Preheat oven to 475°F.

- Make rub out of rosemary, garlic, salt, and pepper.

- Rub olive oil on all sides of each rack of lamb. Rub dry mixture on all sides, pressing to ensure mixture sets in the meat.

- In heavy skillet, on high heat, sear each rack for 3 minutes on each side.

- Place racks in roasting pan, fat side up, and roast at 475°F in center of oven for 14 to 16 minutes for medium rare.

- Transfer rack to warm plate and allow to rest for a few minutes before serving.

- Slice racks into individual servings and arrange on platter.

- Serve with apricot horseradish sauce (recipe follows).

SERVES 12

APRICOT HORSERADISH SAUCE

2 cups apricot preserves

1 cup ground horseradish

½ cup good white wine

1 bay leaf

2 sprigs of thyme

- Combine all ingredients and simmer for 10 minutes.

- Serve with lamb cutlets.

SERVES 12

ALMOND COOKIES

1 cup (2 sticks) unsalted butter

1 cup sugar

1½ teaspoons almond extract

2 eggs

2 cups all-purpose flour

1 teaspoon baking powder

½ cup sliced almonds, coarsely chopped

- Preheat oven to 350°F.

- Cream together butter, sugar, and almond extract. Add eggs, beating well after each addition.

- Sift together flour, baking powder, and almonds. Add to butter mixture.

- Roll dough in waxed paper into long tube shape. Refrigerate at least one hour or until firm enough to work with or freeze until firm enough to work with.

- Slice cookies ¼-inch thick and bake on greased cookie sheet at 350°F about 12 minutes or until light brown.

MAKES 3½ DOZEN

CHOCOLATE DROP COOKIES

1 (12-ounce) package of semisweet chocolate chips

1 can (14 ounces) sweetened condensed milk

1 tablespoon unsalted butter

1 cup sifted all-purpose flour

1 cup chopped pecans

1 teaspoon vanilla

- Preheat oven to 325°F.

- Put first three ingredients in top of double boiler over boiling water and melt.

- Add sifted flour, pecans, and vanilla, mixing well. Remove from heat.

- Cover cookie sheet with foil. Drop dough by teaspoonfuls onto cookie sheet.

- Bake 12 minutes. Let cookies cool on foil slightly before removing.

MAKES 3 TO 4 DOZEN

DONAMIRE FARM

SPRING BRUNCH AFTER THE LEXINGTON BALL

Strawberries with Sour Cream Sauce

Country Ham and Biscuits

Egg and Cheese Casserole

Cheese Grits Soufflé

Orange Swirl Rolls

Banana Bread

Visitors to Donamire Farm are struck not only by the large and impressive home and barns, but also by the complementary landscaping. John Michler of Michler's Gardens and Greenhouses in Lexington designed Donamire's perennial garden, winning the honor award for garden design from the Perennial Plant Association of North America.

Don and Mira Ball have lived on the Old Frankfort Pike farm since the 1960s and have developed the property into a 600-acre showplace that combines a breeding farm with a training center. The training component includes a five-eighths-mile dirt oval and a mile grass track. The couple's horses also race under the name of Donamire.

Don and Mira Ball operate Ball Homes, a major residential building company in Kentucky, with their children Ray Ball, Mike Ball, and Lisa Sharp. The couple have long been active civic leaders and philanthropists in Lexington and have frequently shared Donamire Farm for charitable events. Over the years, as host to the Lexington Foundation Derby Ball and other fund-raisers, the handsomely appointed farm has taken on the trappings of an ancient Roman holiday, a harvest festival, and an elegant "under the sea" soiree. Beneficiaries of these events have included cancer research, education, and care in Kentucky; the Children's Advocacy Center; and Kentucky Educational Television.

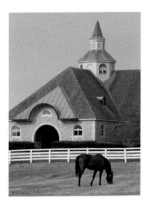

STRAWBERRIES WITH SOUR CREAM SAUCE

1½ quarts fresh strawberries, washed, hulled, and sliced; chill until ready to serve.

- Combine sauce ingredients, blending thoroughly.

- Serve chilled on fresh cut-up strawberries in individual dishes with 2 tablespoons sauce on each.

SOUR CREAM SAUCE

SERVES 8

2 cups sour cream

2 tablespoons dark rum

½ cup plus 2 tablespoons brown sugar

4 teaspoons Grand Marnier

COUNTRY HAM AND BISCUITS

6–8 center cut slices of country ham, cooked

- Preheat oven to 400°F.

- Mix dry ingredients.

BISCUITS

2 teaspoons baking powder

1 cup all-purpose flour

¼ teaspoon salt

¼ cup vegetable shortening

½ cup milk

- Cut shortening into flour mixture until it is blended into size of small peas.

- Add milk and stir until blended.

- Knead dough a few times on lightly floured surface.

- Roll out dough ¼- to ½-inch thick and cut with 1-inch biscuit cutter.

- Place biscuits on greased baking sheet and bake at 400°F for approximately 12 to 15 minutes or until biscuits are light brown.

- Split biscuits in half, cut ham slices to fit, and place on bottom half of biscuit. Top with other half of biscuit. Serve while still warm.

SERVES 10 TO 12

EGG AND CHEESE CASSEROLE

12 slices white bread, crusts removed

2–3 tablespoons unsalted butter, softened

½ cup (1 stick) unsalted butter

½ pound fresh mushrooms, trimmed and sliced

2 cups thinly sliced yellow onions

1½ pounds hot Italian sausage

12–16 ounces sharp cheddar cheese, grated

5 eggs, beaten

2½ cups milk

3 teaspoons Dijon mustard

1 teaspoon dry mustard

1 teaspoon ground nutmeg

1 teaspoon salt (or less)

⅛ teaspoon black pepper

2 tablespoons fresh flat-leaf parsley, finely chopped

- Preheat oven to 350°F.

- Butter bread with softened butter and set aside.

- In a 10-inch or 12-inch skillet, melt ½ cup butter. Sauté mushrooms and onions over medium heat for 5 to 8 minutes, or until tender. Set aside.

- Remove casings from sausage. Brown and break into small bite-sized pieces.

- In a 9x13-inch casserole, layer half of bread (buttered side down), mushroom mixture, sausage, and cheese. Repeat layers, ending with cheese.

- In medium-sized bowl, mix eggs, milk, mustards, nutmeg, salt, and pepper.

- Pour over sausage and cheese casserole. Cover and refrigerate overnight.

- When ready to bake, sprinkle parsley evenly over top of casserole.

- Bake uncovered at 350°F for 1 hour or until bubbly.

SERVES 8 TO 10

CHEESE GRITS SOUFFLÉ

1 cup uncooked grits

2 cups water

2 cups whole milk

4 tablespoons unsalted butter

6 egg yolks, well beaten

6 tablespoons sharp cheddar cheese, grated

Salt and pepper to taste

½ teaspoon paprika

6 egg whites, beaten until stiff peaks form

- Preheat oven to 350°F.

- Cook grits with water and milk according to box directions. Do not overcook grits to hard consistency. Remove from stove.

- Add butter, well-beaten egg yolks, cheese, salt, and paprika.

- Gently fold in beaten egg whites and pour into a well-greased 2½-to-3-quart baking dish.

- Bake at 350°F for 1 hour or until center is firm.

SERVES 8

ORANGE SWIRL ROLLS

ROLLS

2 packages dry yeast

2 cups lukewarm water (110°F)

½ cup sugar

½ cup (1 stick) unsalted butter

⅔ cup nonfat dry milk

2 teaspoons salt

2 eggs

7¼ cups sifted all-purpose flour

FILLING

½ cup (1 stick) unsalted butter, softened

1½ cups sugar

1 tablespoon grated orange zest

ICING

2½ cups sifted confectioner's (powdered) sugar

1 tablespoon grated orange zest

3 tablespoons orange juice

- Sprinkle yeast on lukewarm water in mixing bowl. Stir.

- Add sugar, butter, nonfat dry milk, salt, eggs, and 2 cups flour. Beat with electric mixer about 2 minutes, until smooth.

- Stir in remaining flour until soft dough is formed. Knead in remaining dough for about 10 minutes.

- Let dough rise approximately 1½ hours or until doubles in size. Punch down.

- Divide dough in two. Roll into 7x14-inch rectangles.

- For filling, combine butter, sugar, and orange zest. Divide into two batches. Spread half of mixture on each rectangle.

- Roll into jelly rolls. Cut each roll into 12 pieces.

- Place rolls in 2 greased 9x13-inch pans. Let rolls rise until double in size (about 45 minutes).

- Bake in a preheated 350°F oven for about 25 minutes. Remove rolls from pans immediately. Cool on wire racks.

- Mix icing ingredients together and apply when rolls cool.

MAKES 24 ROLLS

BANANA BREAD

1½ cups sugar

⅔ cup vegetable oil

4 tablespoons buttermilk

1 teaspoon vinegar

2 eggs

1 teaspoon vanilla

¼ teaspoon natural banana flavor

1 cup mashed bananas
(about 2 large bananas)

1 teaspon baking soda,
dissolved in 1 tablespoon of warm
water

1½ cups all-purpose flour

¼ teaspoon salt

½ cup pecans or walnuts, chopped

- Preheat oven to 325 degrees.

- Grease and flour 9-inch loaf pan.

- Cream sugar and oil. In separate small bowl, stir together buttermilk and vinegar; then add to sugar mixture. Add eggs one at a time, making sure to mix well after each addition. Add flavorings and bananas and finally dissolved baking soda.

- In separate bowl, add salt and nuts to flour. Add flour mixture to wet mixture a little at a time. Do not overmix.

- Pour into greased loaf pan. Bake approximately 1 hour until bread tests done (toothpick inserted comes out clean).

- Let bread sit for 1 hour before removing from pan. It can be tricky to remove from pan. Run knife around edge and make sure bread is not sticking to bottom before removing.

MAKES ONE 9-INCH LOAF PAN

HEADLEY-WHITNEY MUSEUM

POST-DERBY BRUNCH

Fruited Salad

Bluegrass Breakfast Cobbler

Crab Cakes with Sun-Dried Tomato Remoulade

Fried Green Tomatoes

Sweet Potato Hash Browns

Meringues with Sliced Strawberries and Whipped Cream

The Headley-Whitney Museum is a living legacy of the artistic tastes of the aesthete responsible for it, the late George Headley. Headley, whose wife was the former Barbara Whitney, traveled the world and collected a unique assemblage of objets d'art. Those on display include a seventeenth-century Italian coral mask of Bacchus, a fourteenth-century French terra cotta pigeon, and a rock crystal chalice. These are housed in the east wing of the two-wing building, constructed in 1964. Headley also created his own art and was especially interested in jewel-encrusted bibelots, decorative objects enjoyed just for their beauty. In 2006 the museum established the International Bibelot Design competition.

On loan from Marylou Whitney is a remarkable quartet of doll houses. Originally commissioned for her daughter, Cornelia, the four doll houses depict the C.V. and Marylou Whitney Lexington house, plus the guest house, artist studio, and pool atrium. Details include replication of the parquet flooring, as well as miniature paintings, a functional harp and piano, and petit point reproductions of the Aubusson carpets.

The museum's shell grotto, added by George Whitney in 1973, features thousands of shells attached to the building's interior, with flooring of coral mined from the Florida Keys. The shell grotto is similar to the Grotto of Thesis built at Versailles by Louis XIV in 1679. The Headley-Whitney library includes some 1,500 volumes, along with a collection of natural objects such as ostrich eggs, turtle shells, and elephant tusks. Reflecting Headley's eclectic tastes, the architecture of the library building combines a sloped Thai roof with Greek columns, English windows, and Georgian moldings. The museum has become a Lexington mainstay and is a popular site for special outdoor events.

FRUITED SALAD

2 oranges, peeled

¾ cup raspberries, washed

¾ cup blueberries, washed

½ red onion, thinly sliced

1 large avocado, peeled and sliced

2 large heads of red Boston lettuce, thoroughly washed and dried

DRESSING

2 tablespoons fresh orange juice

1 tablespoon raspberry vinegar

¼ cup olive oil

2 teaspoons chopped fresh chives

Salt and freshly ground black pepper to taste

- Section oranges, removing pith and seeds. Gently mix with raspberries, blueberries, and onion. Add avocado last. Cover and refrigerate for 30 minutes.

- For dressing, mix all ingredients and whisk until thoroughly blended.

- Tear lettuce into bite-sized pieces and combine in large bowl with fruit, onion, and avocado mixture. Toss all ingredients with dressing to taste.

SERVES 8

BLUEGRASS BREAKFAST COBBLER

FILLING

1 pound bulk spicy pork sausage

3 leeks, washed and chopped

3 Golden Delicious apples, peeled, cored, and cut into chunks

BATTER

½ cup sour cream

2 teaspoons vegetable oil

1 large egg

½ cup yellow cornmeal

½ cup all-purpose flour

1 teaspoon baking soda

½ teaspoon baking powder

1 tablespoon salt

1 tablespoon freshly ground black pepper

½ cup buttermilk

1 cup Swiss cheese, shredded

- Preheat oven to 350°F. Butter a 9x12-inch casserole dish.

- Sauté sausage over medium heat. Add leeks and apples; sauté until soft and golden, about 5 more minutes. With slotted spoon, remove mixture and place in casserole dish.

- Place sour cream, oil, and egg in large bowl and beat together.

- In small bowl, combine dry ingredients. Add dry ingredients alternately with buttermilk to egg mixture. Beat until fully incorporated. Pour batter over sausage mixture and top with cheese.

- Bake at 350°F for 25 minutes or until top is golden and batter is cooked through. Remove from oven and allow to cool 5 to 10 minutes before serving.

SERVES 8

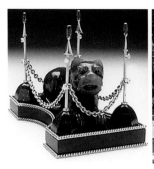

CRAB CAKES WITH SUN-DRIED TOMATO REMOULADE

CRAB CAKES

1 pound crab meat, lump is best

1 egg, beaten

⅓ cup mayonnaise

¼ teaspoon dry mustard

Pinch of black pepper

1 teaspoon Old Bay seasoning

¼ teaspoon celery salt

2 teaspoons Worcestershire sauce

1 tablespoon fresh flat-leaf
parsley, chopped

2 tablespoons red bell pepper,
peeled and chopped

1 tablespoon panko or plain
bread crumbs

2 tablespoons olive oil

2 tablespoons unsalted butter

SUN-DRIED TOMATO REMOULADE

1 quart mayonnaise

3 tablespoons Dijon mustard

2 tablespoons capers

2 teaspoons anchovy paste

2 tablespoons midget dill pickles,
chopped

¼ cup sun-dried tomatoes
in oil, chopped

1 tablespoon fresh tarragon,
chopped

Salt, Tabasco and Worcestershire
sauces to taste

MAKES 1½ QUARTS

- Drain and pick crab meat.

- Mix crab meat and next 9 ingredients
together and form into small cakes.
Dredge in panko or bread crumbs.
Allow to set up in refrigerator for at least
3 hours.

- Heat butter and olive oil in pan. Sauté
cakes until lightly browned on both sides.
Add butter and olive oil in equal amounts
as needed to sauté all cakes.

- Mix all remoulade ingredients well.
Cover and chill overnight.

- Remoulade also goes well with crab cakes,
or with fish or cut vegetables.

MAKES 6 TO 8 SMALL CRAB CAKES

FRIED GREEN TOMATOES

3 firm green tomatoes

¾ cup cornmeal

Salt and pepper to taste

¼ cup canola oil

- Slice tomatoes about ¼-inch thick. Arrange on plate or baking sheet as work surface.

- Sprinkle tomatoes with salt and pepper on one side. Coat same side with cornmeal. Flip tomatoes and repeat procedure.

- Place in heated oil and cook until golden-brown; flip and repeat. Drain on paper towel. Check seasonings.

SERVES 8

SWEET POTATO HASH BROWNS

6 tablespoons butter or olive oil

2 large onions, chopped

6 large sweet potatoes, peeled and coarsely cubed

Salt and freshly ground black pepper to taste

- Add oil or melt butter in large skillet. Add chopped onion and sauté until softened.

- Add potatoes, cover, and cook over low heat until potatoes are tender (15 to 20 minutes).

- Remove cover, adjust heat to medium, and cook until potatoes and onions are browned and crisped. Salt and pepper to taste.

SERVES 8

MERINGUES WITH SLICED STRAWBERRIES AND WHIPPED CREAM

MERINGUES

4 egg whites at room temperature

¼ teaspoon cream of tartar

Pinch of salt

1 teaspoon vanilla

1 cup sugar

SLICED STRAWBERRIES AND WHIPPED CREAM

2 quarts strawberries

1 cup sugar

1 pint whipping cream

1½ tablespoons Framboise (optional)

- Preheat oven to 250°F and line baking sheet with parchment paper.

- Combine egg whites, cream of tartar, salt, and vanilla in mixing bowl. Beat with electric mixer until frothy. Gradually add sugar, beating until stiff peaks form and sugar is dissolved. Mixture should be stiff, dull, and no longer grainy.

- On parchment paper, shape mixture into small individual discs (tartlet size), mounding around edges to make sides higher.

- Bake at 250°F for 1 hour. Turn off heat and allow to dry in oven with door closed for approximately 1 hour.

- Remove and place in airtight container until ready to serve.

- Wash and slice strawberries. Add sugar and toss.

- As you whip cream into soft peaks, add Framboise.

- Place strawberries in center of meringue and serve with a dollop of whipped cream.

MAKES 20 TARTLETS

JUDDMONTE FARMS

SPRING BRUNCH

Gorgonzola Spread

Green Salad with Oranges and Sesame Ginger Vinaigrette

Peasant's Pie

Macaroon Ice Cream with Strawberry Purée

A 2,500-acre state-of-the-art Thoroughbred farm, Juddmonte is the Kentucky division headquarters of the international Thoroughbred breeding operation of Prince Khalid Abdullah of Saudi Arabia. Located just southeast of Lexington, the picturesque Juddmonte Farms is managed by Garrett O'Rourke while Dr. John Chandler is president of Juddmonte USA. Prince Khalid also owns properties abroad. His English headquarters, Banstead Manor, is outside Newmarket.

In the manner of the sportsmen who founded Thoroughbred racing, Prince Khalid breeds horses with the intent of racing his own stock. This program has enjoyed unique success, for he has won each of the five classic races in England and France as well as the classic Belmont Stakes and the Kentucky Oaks in this country. His homebred 2003 Belmont Stakes winner, Empire Maker, is one of three stallions at Juddmonte, along with Aptitude and Mizzen Mast.

Prince Khalid began breeding such classic winners after he developed a prime broodmare band through purchases of stock at Keeneland and elsewhere. He has won the Epsom Derby in England with Quest for Fame (1990) and Commander in Chief (1993), plus France's climactic race, the Prix de l'Arc de Triomphe, with Rainbow Quest (1985), Dancing Brave (1986), and Rail Link (2006). Prince Khalid also has the singular distinction of having bred the stallion with the highest number of stakes winners in history, the prolific internationalist Danehill.

Juddmonte also has supported the best races in America, where its homebreds have won Breeders' Cup races with Banks Hill and Intercontinental as well as ten Eclipse Awards. Four Eclipses were presented to Prince Khalid as leading owner and leading breeder. An integral part of the Kentucky Thoroughbred scene, Juddmonte has hosted the Thoroughbred Owners and Breeders Association annual awards evening.

GORGONZOLA SPREAD

6 ounces Gorgonzola cheese

½ cup (1 stick) unsalted butter, softened

⅓ cup chopped pecans

1 loaf (baguette) French bread

- Combine cheese, butter, and pecans.

- Slice bread into ¼-inch thick pieces.

- Spread mixture on each piece and bake in 350°F oven until bubbly.

SERVES 8

GREEN SALAD WITH ORANGES AND SESAME GINGER VINAIGRETTE

SALAD

3 heads Boston lettuce
(red Boston is more colorful),
washed and dried

3 naval oranges, sectioned
and membrane removed
(reserve juice)

2 avocados, peeled and sliced

¾ cup sliced almonds, toasted

3 scallions, thinly sliced

SESAME GINGER VINAIGRETTE

4 tablespoons rice wine vinegar

2 teaspoons sesame seeds

4 tablespoons soy sauce

2 cloves garlic, minced

4 tablespoons honey

2 tablespoons crystallized ginger

1 teaspoon sesame oil

8 tablespoons canola oil

Juice from segmented oranges

- Tear lettuce into bite-sized pieces and place on individual salad plates or in large bowl.

- Arrange orange segments and avocado slices on top of lettuce and sprinkle with almonds and green onions.

- Mix all dressing ingredients in jar and shake to blend. Drizzle sesame ginger vinaigrette on greens.

SERVES 8

PEASANT'S PIE

6 tablespoons unsalted butter

4 cans artichoke hearts,
    quartered and drained

2¼ pounds fresh mushrooms, halved

2 teaspoons minced garlic

6 tablespoons fresh flat-leaf
    parsley, chopped

2 (10x15-inch) puff pastry sheets

2¼ pounds Swiss (or mozzarella)
    cheese, grated

2 pounds medium shrimp, cooked
    and peeled

Salt to taste

Parmesan cheese, grated for garnish

Chopped fresh flat-leaf parsley
    for garnish

- Melt butter on medium heat and add artichoke hearts and mushrooms. Cook until tender.

- Add minced garlic and parsley. Allow to cool and drain liquid.

- Grease baking sheet. Preheat oven to 450°F.

- Roll out pastry sheets according to directions on package.

- Spread half of cheese, shrimp, and mushroom mixture in center of each pastry sheet. Moisten edges of pastry with water and pull corners together around mixture, twisting to tie a knot on top. Press edges together to seal the pie. Repeat this step to make second pie.

- Place pies on baking sheet.

- Bake at 450°F for 15 minutes. Reduce heat to 375°F and bake for 30 to 40 minutes.

- Sprinkle Parmesan cheese and fresh parsley on top.

2 PIES SERVE 8

MACAROON ICE CREAM WITH STRAWBERRY PURÉE

2 cups crumbled almond macaroons

3 tablespoons orange-flavored
    liqueur

1 quart vanilla ice cream, softened

1 cup heavy cream, whipped

¼ cup chopped toasted almonds

STRAWBERRY PURÉE

1 quart fresh strawberries,
    washed and halved

⅓ cup sugar

3 tablespoons amaretto liqueur

- Stir macaroons and orange liqueur into softened ice cream.

- Gently fold in whipped cream and pour into 1 quart soufflé dish. Cover dish and freeze until firm, about 4 hours or overnight.

- To serve, remove ice cream from freezer and let stand at room temperature 10 to 15 minutes, until soft enough to scoop. While ice cream is softening, simmer the strawberries and sugar in saucepan over low heat until fruit is soft but not mushy. Remove from heat and add amaretto liqueur.

- Spoon ice cream into individual dishes and top with almonds. Serve with warm strawberry sauce. Ice cream can be refrozen in dishes if prepared ahead and softened before serving.

SERVES 8

KEENELAND

A DAY AT THE RACES

Kentucky Burgoo

Grilled Asparagus in Sweet Balsamic Syrup

Blue Cheese Stuffed New Potatoes

Rosemary Garlic Beef Tenderloin with Horseradish Sauce

Keeneland Bread Pudding and Bourbon Sauce

Located in the heart of Central Kentucky, Keeneland combines high-stakes commerce and genteel sporting tradition. From its inception in 1936, Keeneland was intended to cultivate an enduring appreciation and respect for the Thoroughbred.

As the world's largest Thoroughbred auction company, Keeneland conducts horse sales that annually exceed a half-billion dollars — two-thirds of the North American market's gross sales. Its racing program, conducted every April and October, offers some of the richest purses — and the most competitive racing — of any other track on the continent. In 2006 Keeneland became one of the pioneering tracks to install Polytrack, a synthetic surface safer for horses and riders than traditional dirt. Thus, the bastion of tradition also showed an innovative ability to provide the competitors the best possible care.

Further enhancing its reputation as a leader in the Thoroughbred industry, Keeneland strictly adheres to the best customs of the sport. As one of the founders, Hal Price Headley, said, "We want a place where those who love horses can come and picnic with us and thrill to the sport of the horses racing." The words ring as true today as they did when Headley first said them.

Unique in corporate structure, Keeneland is a tax-paying entity that also is non-dividend paying. Thus, Keeneland, a National Historic Landmark, is "a for-profit company with a not-for-profit mission." Its directors serve without remuneration and profits are funneled back into the operation in the form of higher purses for horse owners and capital improvements to the facility. Also, Keeneland's contributions to charitable, education, and research organizations through the years have exceeded $15 million.

KENTUCKY BURGOO

3 pounds beef stew meat, cubed

1 teaspoon each: ground thyme and dried sage

1 teaspoon garlic, chopped

1 teaspoon fresh oregano, chopped

1 (7-ounce) can tomato purée

2 pounds fresh or frozen okra, sliced

1 tablespoon beef base

1 teaspoon Worcestershire sauce

3–4 tablespoons vegetable oil

Salt and pepper to taste

1 cup sherry wine

1 cup celery, diced

1 cup red wine

1 cup onion, diced

3 pounds potatoes, diced

1 (12-ounce) can diced tomatoes in juice

1 tablespoon chicken base

Slurry of cornstarch

2 packages frozen mixed vegetables

- Brown stew meat with herbs and garlic in oil.

- Add remaining ingredients, mixing well, and cover with water.

- Bring to boil; then reduce heat and simmer for 3 hours or until meat is tender.

- Adjust seasoning and thicken with slurry of cornstarch, if necessary.

SERVES 10 TO 12

GRILLED ASPARAGUS IN SWEET BALSAMIC SYRUP

70 medium asparagus spears

⅓ cup kosher salt

4 tablespoons olive oil

SWEET BALSAMIC SYRUP

4 cups balsamic vinegar

- Cover asparagus with olive oil and salt. Let sit for at least 1 hour.

- On outdoor grill, roast asparagus in a vegetable basket over medium heat until tender and a bit seared. Asparagus can be cooked on stove in grill pan.

- Heat vinegar on stove until reduced by half to form syrup. (This can be made ahead and reheated.)

- Pour sweet balsamic syrup over asparagus before serving.

SERVES 10 TO 12

BLUE CHEESE STUFFED NEW POTATOES

24 red new potatoes

2 cups crumbled blue cheese

¼ cup fresh chives, chopped

Salt to taste

1 teaspoon white pepper

- Boil potatoes in water until tender but with skins unbroken. Let them cool.

- Cut off tops and hollow potatoes out, leaving some potato in the cavity. Keep tops.

- Put spooned-out potato in bowl and add blue cheese, pepper, and chives. Mix together and correct seasoning.

- Carefully put potato mixture back into skins.

- Bake at 325°F until cheese melts.

- Serve with tops on.

SERVES 10 TO 12

ROSEMARY GARLIC BEEF TENDERLOIN WITH HORSERADISH SAUCE

1 beef tenderloin, trimmed and cleaned

MARINADE

3 tablespoons garlic, chopped

1 tablespoon cracked black pepper

1 cup vegetable oil

½ cup balsamic vinegar

2 tablespoons kosher salt

¼ cup fresh rosemary, chopped

HORSERADISH SAUCE

½ cup mayonnaise

⅓ cup prepared horseradish, drained

½ cup heavy cream, whipped

Tabasco sauce to taste

⅛ teaspoon dry mustard

Worcestershire sauce to taste

- Combine marinade ingredients in bowl.

- Rub mixture on beef and marinate in refrigerator for at least 6 hours.

- Before cooking, allow tenderloin to come to just above room temperature.

- Preheat oven to 500°F. Place tenderloin in roasting pan and insert meat thermometer. Reduce oven temperature to 350°F when you put tenderloin in. Bake for 20 minutes or until meat thermometer registers 120°F. Meat will be rare but will continue to cook a little after you remove it from oven.

- Let tenderloin sit for about 15 to 20 minutes before slicing.

- For sauce, combine mayonnaise and whipped cream.

- Stir in dry mustard and horseradish.

- Season lightly with Tabasco and Worcestershire sauces. Serve with tenderloin.

SERVES 10 TO 12

KEENELAND BREAD PUDDING AND BOURBON SAUCE

1 tablespoon butter, softened

2 cups sugar

¼ teaspoon salt

1 tablespoon cinnamon

6 cups whole milk

8 large eggs, beaten

1 tablespoon vanilla

12 cups densely packed and cubed day-old French bread, crust removed

1 cup golden raisins

BOURBON SAUCE

1 pound unsalted butter

2 pounds powdered (confectioner's) sugar

1 cup bourbon

- Preheat oven to 325°F.

- Generously grease 3-quart ovenproof dish with softened butter.

- In large bowl, combine sugar, salt, and cinnamon. Whisk milk into dry ingredients until sugar is dissolved. Add eggs and vanilla, stirring well to incorporate all ingredients.

- Soak bread in mixture for half-hour.

- Pour into buttered ovenproof dish.

- Sprinkle raisins on top and press into bread.

- Bake at 325°F for 1 hour and 15 minutes or until firm to touch and golden-brown.

- For sauce, soften butter to room temperature and add powdered sugar. Beat with electric mixer until combined.

- Whip bourbon into mix until it achieves frosting consistency. Ladle sauce over hot bread pudding. Sauce will "melt" on its own.

SERVES 16

SHADOWLAWN FARM

SPRING SUPPER

Oven Zucchini Chips with Blue Cheese Blender Dip

Shrimp Creole with Rice

Braided Bread

Sticky Toffee Pudding

Shadowlawn Farm in scenic Midway, Kentucky, is owned by business-man Tracy Farmer, who has had much success with his horse racing endeavors since he bought the farm in 1993. Farmer has owned such winners as Albert the Great, Sun King, Hidden Lake, and Commentator. The farm, itself, though might be best known as the site of the 1988 television miniseries *Bluegrass*, starring Cheryl Ladd.

Shadowlawn Farm started out as part of a larger farm owned by W.J. Walden, who began buying broodmares in the late 1930s and early '40s, when the prices were low. Walden soon set apart a portion of his farm as a breeding operation. He later turned the farm over to his son Ben P. Walden, with whom he had been partners for many years.

The farm was leased in the 1970s to Harry Rainer and Dr. William Lockridge, who ended up buying the property. In 1980 the two men dissolved their partnership, with Shadowlawn going to Rainer. The farm later encountered some financial problems but was set back on track when Farmer purchased the 135-acre property .

Formerly the chairman of several drugstores and dry cleaners in ten states, Farmer is now involved in banking, commercial real estate, and horses. He donated $2 million to the University of Kentucky for the creation of a center for environmental study. He also served on the UK's board of trustees for twelve years.

OVEN ZUCCHINI CHIPS

¼ cup fine bread crumbs
   or panko flakes

½ cup grated fresh
   Parmesan cheese

3 tablespoons milk

¼ teaspoon seasoned salt

¼ teaspoon garlic salt

⅛ teaspoon freshly ground
   black pepper

Cooking spray

2½ zucchinis (2–3 small ones),
   sliced ¼-inch thick

- Preheat oven to 425°F.

- Combine first five ingredients in medium bowl, stirring with a whisk.

- Place milk in shallow bowl. Dip zucchini slices in milk; then dredge in bread-crumb mixture.

- Place slices on ovenproof wire rack coated with cooking spray. Place rack on a baking sheet.

- Bake at 425°F for 25 minutes or until browned and crisp. Do not turn. Serve immediately.

SERVES 6

BLUE CHEESE BLENDER DIP

1 (8-ounce) carton sour cream

1 (8-ounce) package cream cheese

4 ounces blue cheese, crumbled

Worcestershire sauce to taste

Lemon juice to taste

2 large green bell peppers

- Place sour cream, cream cheese, blue cheese, Worcestershire sauce, and lemon juice in blender.

- Blend until mixture is smooth and then chill until ready to serve.

- Remove top and seeds from bell peppers and spoon dip into peppers for serving as a dip for zucchini chips.

MAKES 2 CUPS

SHRIMP CREOLE WITH RICE

2 strips bacon

2 tablespoons oil

1 green bell pepper,
coarsely chopped

2 medium-sized onions,
coarsely chopped

1½ cups celery, chopped

1 quart can tomatoes,
slightly broken

1 (6-ounce) can tomato paste

3–6 drops Tabasco sauce

2 tablespoons Worcestershire sauce

Salt and pepper

2 pounds raw shrimp, shelled
and deveined

- Fry bacon until crisp and remove from pan, reserving drippings in pan. Crumble bacon and put aside.

- Add oil to bacon drippings. Cook onions, green pepper, and celery until tender.

- Add tomatoes and tomato paste and allow mixture to simmer for 45 minutes. Sauce may need a small amount of water but should remain thick.

- Stir in Tabasco sauce, Worcestershire sauce, and salt and pepper. Add shrimp and cook until shrimp turn pink. Serve over rice and garnish with crumbled bacon.

SERVES 6

BRAIDED BREAD

5½ cups bread flour

2 packages active dry yeast

1 tablespoon sugar

1 teaspoon salt

2 tablespoons unsalted butter, softened

2½ cups hot tap water

Sesame seeds

1 egg, beaten

- Preheat oven to 375°F.

- Combine 2 cups flour, yeast, sugar, and salt in large mixing bowl. Stir to blend and add butter. Slowly pour hot water in bowl and beat with electric mixer for one minute.

- Stir in remaining flour with wooden spoon to make a soft dough. You may need more flour (dough should leave the side of the bowl).

- Turn out onto floured surface and shape into a ball. Knead the dough. Cover dough with plastic wrap and a towel and allow to rest 20 minutes.

- Punch down, divide dough into 6 equal portions, and shape each sixth into a long strip. Make two braids by laying 3 strips side by side and braid starting in the middle. Turn dough around and braid from other side down to the outer edges.

- Place braids on a greased baking sheet and brush lightly with oil. Cover loosely with plastic wrap and place in refrigerator for 2 to 24 hours.

- Remove from refrigerator and allow to sit for 10 minutes. Brush with beaten egg and sprinkle with sesame seeds. Bake at 375°F for 30 to 35 minutes.

MAKES 2 LOAVES OF BREAD

STICKY TOFFEE PUDDING

½ cup (1 stick) unsalted butter softened, plus extra for greasing

¾ cup brown sugar

4 medium eggs, lightly beaten

1 cup self-rising flour

1 teaspoon baking soda

1 cup finely chopped dates

2 tablespoons Camp Coffee Essence* (extract)

1¼ cups boiling water

1 cup walnut or pecan halves, optional

TOPPING

4 tablespoons heavy cream

¾ cup brown sugar

½ cup (1 stick) unsalted butter

BUTTERSCOTCH SAUCE

1 cup Lyle's Golden Syrup

½ stick softened butter

½ cup brown sugar

Finely grated zest of 2 oranges

2–3 drops vanilla extract

Heavy cream, whipped (optional)

- Preheat oven to 350°F and prepare a 9-inch or 10-inch square baking pan. Line pan with two sheets of wax paper, overlapping sides and then greasing with melted butter. Place this pan on a baking sheet with sides for spillage.

- Cream butter and sugar in a bowl. Slowly add beaten eggs one at a time.

- Sift flour and baking soda and fold into mixture. Add finely chopped dates.

- Mix coffee extract with boiling water and pour into mixture (which will begin to bubble). Mixture should be wet and lumpy. Continue to mix with large spoon until batter is smooth but runny. If using nuts, add them into mixture now.

- Pour batter into prepared pan set on baking sheet. Bake in oven approximately 1 to 1½ hours or until tester is clean. This part can be prepared several hours to one day ahead of time. Cover with foil after cooling.

- Just before pudding is ready, combine topping ingredients in small saucepan and bring to boil. Remove cooked pudding from oven and pour topping over it. Brown under broiler.

- For butterscotch sauce, place all sauce ingredients in small saucepan over low heat and whisk until blended. For richer sauce add a couple of tablespoons of whipped cream.

- Serve pudding cut into squares with butterscotch sauce and dollop of whipped cream on top.

*Camp Coffee essence or extract may be acquired by calling (800) 749-0739.

SERVES 8 TO 16

MARYLOU WHITNEY STABLES

DINNER AT WHITNEY HOUSE
AFTER OPENING DAY AT KEENELAND

Caviar Canapés

Broccoli Ring

Potato Rolls

Best Beef Tenderloin with Béarnaise Sauce

Fried Corn

Mocha-Macaroon Freeze

The Whitney name is synonymous with Bluegrass hospitality. For years Marylou Whitney has hosted elegant parties for friends, royalty, and celebrities, sharing the elegance and ambience of her historic house, Maple Hill, and embracing a traditional approach to the Turf. The Whitney name also is synonymous with American racing. Whitney's late husband, Cornelius Vanderbilt Whitney, continued the family stable started by his grandfather, William Collins Whitney, in the latter years of the nineteenth century.

The Whitney dynasty has raced more stakes winners than any other American family. W.C. Whitney was succeeded by son Harry Payne Whitney, who won the Kentucky Derby with the filly Regret in 1915. Harry Payne Whitney passed along to C.V. Whitney the champions Equipoise and Top Flight as young horses, and C.V. built upon that legacy. In addition to Belmont Stakes winners Phalanx and Counterpoint, the best horses he bred included champions First Flight, Silver Spoon, and Career Boy. More than one hundred years after the family's first classic win Mrs. Whitney and her husband, John Hendrickson, added their own chapters to the family tradition of classic victories. In 2004 Mrs. Whitney's homebred Birdstone won the Belmont Stakes, the final race in the Triple Crown. Birdstone also won the Travers Stakes at Saratoga Springs, where Mrs. Whitney maintains another beloved house, Cady Hill.

Mrs. Whitney also raced the three-year-old filly champion Bird Town, whose victories included the 2003 Kentucky Oaks. Again, this was tradition being served, for C.V. Whitney himself raced four Kentucky Oaks winners.

CAVIAR CANAPÉS

10 slices very thin white bread

3 large ripe tomatoes

¾ cup mayonnaise

1 small onion, minced

2 jars caviar (white fish)

4 eggs, hard-boiled

Fresh lemon juice

- With 2- or 3-inch biscuit cutter, cut rounds from bread slices and toast lightly under the broiler.

- Peel and slice tomatoes.

- Put a thin layer of mayonnaise on each bread round and then add tomato slice.

- Sprinkle tomato with minced onion and then place mound of caviar on top.

- Grate egg yolks and sprinkle on caviar. Top with small dollop of mayonnaise.

- Squirt a few drops of fresh lemon juice on top.

- To serve as first course, garnish plate with fresh salad greens and place canapé on plate with lemon wedge.

SERVES 10

BROCCOLI RING

3 tablespoons butter

3 tablespoons all-purpose flour

1 cup milk

¼ teaspoon salt

6 eggs, separated

2 cups chopped, cooked broccoli florets

6 tablespoons chopped celery

3 tablespoons minced onion

Juice of ½ lemon

1 cup mayonnaise

- Melt butter over low heat and blend in flour.

- Slowly stir in milk, add salt, and cook, stirring constantly until smooth.

- Beat egg yolks and stir into sauce. Add broccoli, celery, onion, and lemon juice. Mix well.

- Cool mixture and stir in mayonnaise.

- Beat egg whites until stiff and fold into broccoli mixture.

- Spoon into greased 2-quart ring mold. Set mold in pan of water 1-inch deep and bake at 350°F for one hour. Carefully run a knife around inner and outer edge of mold, shake slightly, place serving plate over mold, and flip over so mold is on top of plate.

SERVES 8 TO 10

POTATO ROLLS

1 pint milk

½ cup (1 stick) unsalted butter, softened

½ cup sugar

¾ teaspoon salt

½ cup boiled potato, mashed

1 cake or package dry yeast

1 teaspoon baking powder

½ teaspoon baking soda

6–6½ cups all-purpose flour

1–2 teaspoons softened butter to spread over dough

1 stick butter for dipping rolls

½ cup sugar (optional) for dipping rolls

- Pour milk into saucepan. Bring milk to boiling point then cool and skim surface.

- In mixing bowl, cream butter, sugar, and salt, and then add mashed potato.

- In a separate bowl, dissolve yeast in 1 cup of the cooled milk and stir in baking powder and baking soda. Add rest of milk and stir to combine.

- Pour milk into creamed butter mixture and blend well.

- Mix in enough flour (6–6½ cups) to make a stiff dough.

- Put dough in large bowl. Spread thin film of softened butter over top of dough, cover bowl with plastic wrap, and refrigerate at least 4 hours or up to 5 days.

- To bake: Grease 2-inch muffin tins. Knead dough well on floured surface, approximately 5 minutes.

- Pull off amount of dough to make a nickel-sized ball; dip top in melted butter and then in sugar (optional). Put 3 balls in each greased 2-inch muffin tin cup.

- Cover tins loosely with wax paper and let stand 2½ hours before baking. (You can make these earlier, refrigerate, then remove, and let stand 2½ hours.) Preheat oven to 425°F.

- Bake 7 to 8 minutes or until golden brown.

YIELDS 24 TO 30 ROLLS

BEST BEEF TENDERLOIN

6–7 pound beef tenderloin, trimmed

3 tablespoons olive oil

1½ teaspoons onion powder

1½ tablespoons ground kosher salt

¾ teaspoon cumin

1½ teaspoons freshly ground black pepper

¾ teaspoon nutmeg

1 teaspoon ground red pepper

- Rub olive oil over tenderloin; then rub with combined seasonings.

- Refrigerate for at least 6 hours or overnight.

- Remove meat from refrigerator and allow to sit for 20 minutes.

- Cook on grill over medium heat for 10 to 15 minutes on each of three sides.

- Wrap meat tightly in aluminum foil and allow to rest for 15 to 20 minutes before slicing.

- May be served hot or cold. Serve with béarnaise sauce (recipe below).

SERVES 8 TO 10

BÉARNAISE SAUCE

3 tablespoons chopped shallots

¼ cup tarragon white wine vinegar

½ cup white wine

1 teaspoon dried tarragon

2 egg yolks

1 cup butter, melted and hot

Salt to taste

- Boil first four ingredients in saucepan until there is just a film left at the bottom of pan, almost no liquid.

- Place reduced liquid in food processor. Blend in egg yolks and then, with motor running, slowly add hot butter in thin stream.

- Blend until thick and add salt to taste.

MAKES APPROXIMATELY 1½ CUPS

FRIED CORN

1 dozen ears of corn

½ cup butter

½ red bell pepper, diced

Dash of cayenne pepper

½ green bell pepper, diced

Salt and pepper to taste

- Cut kernels from corn and scrape ears to extract "milk."

- Melt butter in large sauté pan, add diced peppers, and sauté for 1 minute.

- Add corn, extracted milk, and seasonings.

- Simmer for 20 to 30 minutes, adding a little water if necessary to prevent sticking.

SERVES 8 TO 10

MOCHA-MACAROON FREEZE

1½ pounds almond macaroons

¾–1 cup dark rum

2 quarts mocha or coffee ice cream, slightly softened

2 pints whipping cream

Fresh mint leaves for garnish

- Soak macaroons in dark rum for 20 to 30 minutes.

- Cover bottom and sides of Revere-style bowl with macaroons. Press them around inside of bowl to within 1 inch of rim.

- Put 1 quart of slightly softened ice cream in bowl and cover with layer of rum-soaked macaroons. Add remaining quart of softened ice cream on top. This dessert can be made days ahead and kept in freezer.

- When ready to serve, top with stiffly beaten whipped cream and crumbled macaroons. Garnish with fresh mint leaves.

SERVES 10

SUMMER

ASHVIEW FARM

SUMMER SUPPER POOLSIDE

Mexican Tapenade

Tossed Lettuces with Green Vinaigrette

Fire and Ice Tomatoes

Grilled Corn

Steamed Lobster with Citrus Sauce

Grilled Skirt Steak with Peaches

Blueberry-Raspberry Crumble with Vanilla Ice Cream

The 350-acre Ashview Farm, owned by Wayne G. Lyster III and his wife, Muffy, is located near Versailles, Kentucky. Ashview was purchased by the Lysters in 1978 and is home to approximately fifty broodmares and their offspring.

French General Marquis Calmes, a great friend of General Lafayette during the American Revolution, originally owned the land on which the farm is situated. Calmes is responsible for laying out the town of Versailles and naming it after the French palace. He is buried in a stone mausoleum that he built and that rests in the middle of a paddock on Ashview Farm.

The main house was built in the 1840s and is considered a Greek Revival-style farmhouse.

Through the years of the Lysters' ownership, Ashview has bred approximately thirty stakes winners, including 2001 Breeders' Cup Juvenile winner and world champion Johannesburg. Unbeaten in seven races at two that year, Johannesburg had the distinction of winning grade/group I events in four countries — the United States, England, Ireland, and France.

MEXICAN TAPENADE

3 (3.5-ounce) cans chopped
　ripe black olives, drained

3 (14.5-ounce) cans whole toma-
　toes, drained, seeded,
　and chopped

3 (4-ounce) cans chopped green
　chilies, drained

8–9 scallions, chopped

3 cloves garlic, minced

1 tablespoon olive oil

1 tablespoon red wine vinegar

1½ teaspoons freshly ground
　black pepper

Salt to taste

- Make a day ahead.

- Combine ingredients, stirring well with a spoon, and chill overnight.

- Mixture may need to be drained slightly before serving with
  tortilla chips.

SERVES 15 TO 20

TOSSED LETTUCES WITH GREEN VINAIGRETTE

SALAD

1 head iceberg lettuce,
　shredded

1 head radicchio, shredded

1 head Romaine lettuce,
　shredded

GREEN VINAIGRETTE

1 medium onion, diced

⅛ teaspoon freshly ground
　black pepper

2 medium cloves garlic, chopped

2 cups canola oil

1 tablespoon salt

¾ cup cider vinegar

2 tablespoons sugar

¼ cup water

¼ teaspoon Dijon mustard

2 teaspoons flat-leaf parsley

¼ teaspoon paprika

2 teaspoons celery salt

- Mix all ingredients in blender or food
  processor until well blended. Vinaigrette
  lasts several weeks in refrigerator.

- Toss lettuces and dressing together just
  before serving.

SERVES 10

FIRE AND ICE TOMATOES

6 large tomatoes, sliced medium thick (¼ inch)

1 large green bell pepper, sliced into thin rings

1 large red onion, sliced into thin rings

½ cup freshly chopped flat-leaf parsley

MARINADE

¾ cup cider vinegar

1½ teaspoons mustard seed

¼ cup water

½ teaspoon salt

4½ teaspoons sugar

⅛ teaspoon black pepper

1½ teaspoons celery salt

⅛ teaspoon cayenne

- In saucepan, combine all marinade ingredients. Boil one minute. Allow to cool.

- In large shallow serving dish, alternate tomato slices with pepper and onion rings. Pour marinade over all and refrigerate several hours before serving.

- Garnish with parsley.

SERVES 10 TO 12

GRILLED CORN

10–15 ears fresh corn

- Soak corn in shucks for one hour.

- Cook in shucks on covered grill for 20 to 30 minutes. Turn twice during cooking.

- Remove from heat. Allow to cool long enough to peel shucks off of corn.

- Serve with drawn butter and coarse salt.

SERVES 10 TO 15

STEAMED LOBSTER WITH CITRUS SAUCE

8 medium-sized lobsters

2 large pots of boiling water
(6–8 quarts of water in each)

CITRUS SAUCE

1 cup dry white wine

2 tablespoons fresh lime juice

4 tablespoons sliced shallots

3 teaspoons fresh lemon juice

2 fresh thyme sprigs

1 cup chilled butter, diced

½ cup heavy cream

2 teaspoons sea salt

2 tablespoons fresh orange juice

Dash of Tabasco sauce, to taste

- Bring water to rolling boil.

- Plunge lobsters head first into water.

- Boil for approximately 10 minutes.

- Remove from water at once and drain in sink or large bucket.

- In small sauce pan, combine wine, shallots, and thyme. Bring to boil and simmer over medium-low heat until liquid is reduced by two-thirds.

- Add cream and simmer 5 minutes.

- Add orange, lime, and lemon juices. Turn heat to low and add butter, a few pieces at a time. Whisk constantly until butter is completely incorporated. Boiling will ruin the sauce.

- Season with salt and Tabasco to taste.

- Strain and keep warm until serving.

- Crack lobster claws, split tail, and serve with citrus sauce.

SERVES 6 TO 8

BLUEBERRY-RASPBERRY CRUMBLE

2 pints blueberries

2 pints raspberries

4 tablespoons instant tapioca

2 tablespoons lemon juice

1¼ cups sugar

2 tablespoons lime juice

CRUMBLE TOPPING

6 tablespoons unsalted
butter, softened

¼ cup packed light brown sugar

¼ teaspoon lemon juice

1 cup all-purpose flour

Pinch of salt

- Preheat oven to 375°F.

- Rinse berries and mix in instant tapioca. Let stand for 10 minutes and then add remaining ingredients, mix well, and pour into 9x12-inch Pyrex baking dish.

- For topping, combine butter, brown sugar, and lemon juice with electric mixer. Beat on medium speed until creamy.

- Stir in flour and salt. Work mixture with fingers until it forms coarse crumbs ranging in size from peas to gum balls. Add crumble topping to Pyrex dish.

- Bake until topping turns golden-brown and bubbles, 30 to 35 minutes.

- Serve with vanilla ice cream.

SERVES 8

GRILLED SKIRT STEAK WITH PEACHES

6 garlic cloves

3 small bay leaves

3 small shallots

2 jalapeños, halved and seeded

Finely grated zest and juice
   of 3 lemons

6 tablespoons soy sauce

1½ teaspoons chopped thyme

½ cup, plus 1 tablespoon
   canola oil

Salt and freshly ground
   black pepper

4½ pounds skirt steak,
   cut into 6 pieces

3 tablespoons Dijon mustard

1½ cups boiling water

6 tablespoons honey

1½ teaspoons cinnamon

4½ teaspoons finely grated fresh
   ginger

12 peaches, halved and pitted

- In a blender, purée the garlic, bay leaves, shallots, jalapeños, lemon zest and juice, soy sauce, and thyme until combined. With the blender on, slowly add ½ cup of canola oil and purée until smooth. Season with salt and pepper.

- Pour half of the marinade into a shallow dish, add the skirt steak, and turn to coat. Let the skirt steak stand for 20 minutes.

- Add Dijon mustard to remaining marinade and blend. Transfer marinade to small bowl.

- Light the grill.

- In small saucepan, combine boiling water with honey, cinnamon, and ginger and let stand 5 minutes. Transfer mixture to a bowl; then add remaining 1 tablespoon of oil and peaches.

- Scrape marinade off skirt steak. Generously season steaks with salt and pepper. Grill over high heat 6 to 7 minutes, turning once for medium-rare meat.

- At the same time, grill peach halves, turning them frequently, until charred in spots and softened, approximately 8 minutes.

- Cut peaches into wedges and thinly slice steaks. Transfer to plates and serve with marinade on the side.

SERVES 8

CALUMET FARM

Basil and Tomato Feta Bruschetta

Cucumber Avocado Soup

Cheese Soufflé

Green Beans with Zucchini

Raspberry Walnut Salad

The "Best" Cream Cheese Pound Cake with Peaches

Since the 1920s, travelers on the road between Lexington and points west have marveled at the loveliness of Calumet Farm. The prototype for the post-card image of the Bluegrass horse farm, Calumet offers a vista of rolling green fields, glistening white fences, and majestic barns while well-bred mares and their foals graze or play nonchalantly. In the distance sits a handsome mansion.

The farm is owned by the family of the dashing late Polish entrepreneur Henryk de Kwiatkowski, whose flourishing stable of the 1980s and '90s included Horse of the Year Conquistador Cielo. De Kwiatkowski attained hero status in the Bluegrass when he rescued Calumet in 1992, purchasing it at public auction for $17 million and promising "not to change one blade of grass." He was good to his word, and his family and trustees have followed suit.

The financial collapse prompting the auction stood in stark contrast to Calumet's glory days. Having been developed as a Standardbred farm in 1924 by William Monroe Wright, Calumet was converted to Thoroughbreds by the founder's son, Warren Sr. For a prolonged era Calumet dominated American racing. It led owners in purse earnings twelve times between 1941 and 1961 and led breeders fourteen times between 1947 and 1957. Wright and his trainers, Ben and Jimmy Jones, coveted the Kentucky Derby. So did Mrs. Lucille Wright, who after her husband's death operated the farm with her second husband, Admiral Gene Markey.

Eventually, Calumet set the record for breeding Derby winners, with nine, and for owning them, with eight. Many of Calumet's champions are represented in the farm's cemetery, watched over by a statue of the great Calumet stallion Bull Lea.

BASIL AND TOMATO FETA BRUSCHETTA

1 loaf (baguette) French bread, cut into ½-inch thick slices

½ cup plus 1 tablespoon olive oil

1 pound tomatoes, chopped (about 2 ½ cups)

4 ounces feta cheese with basil and tomato, crumbled

½ cup red onion, finely chopped

1 tablespoon fresh flat-leaf parsley, chopped

1 tablespoon ripe black olives, pitted and chopped

¼ teaspoon black pepper

- Preheat oven to broil, place bread on cookie sheet, and broil on both sides until lightly browned.

- Brush bread slices lightly with olive oil.

- Combine tomatoes, 1 tablespoon olive oil, feta cheese, onion, parsley, olives, and pepper.

- Spoon about 2 teaspoons of tomato mixture onto each toast slice just before serving.

- This dish can be prepared several hours before serving if you keep cooled toast slices in airtight container and tomato mixture in refrigerator. Be sure and bring tomato mixture to room temperature before putting it on toasted bread.

SERVES 6

CUCUMBER AVOCADO SOUP

2 large cucumbers, peeled, seeded, and coarsely chopped

2 cups sour cream or plain yogurt

2 small, ripe avocados

6 tablespoons fresh lime juice

4 scallions, chopped

Dashes of Tabasco sauce

2 cups chicken stock

Salt to taste

Snipped chives for garnish

- Blend all ingredients, except chives, in food processor or blender until smooth.

- Chill for several hours and serve in demitasse cups.

- Sprinkle chives for garnish.

- Serve as first course.

SERVES 6

CHEESE SOUFFLÉ

¼ cup Parmesan cheese, finely grated

6 tablespoons unsalted butter plus additional butter to grease dish

6 tablespoons flour

1½ cups whole milk, warmed

1 teaspoon salt

2 teaspoons fresh tarragon, chopped

1 teaspoon Tabasco sauce

10 large egg yolks

2 cups sharp cheddar cheese, grated

12 large egg whites

- Preheat oven to 350°F.

- Make collar out of brown paper, 3½ to 4 inches wide, for 2-quart soufflé dish. Butter collar and dish. Sprinkle dish and collar with finely grated Parmesan cheese. Secure collar around dish with kitchen twine so collar rises about 3 or 3½ inches above dish.

- Prepare cream sauce by melting butter over low heat. Add flour and cook several minutes. Stir in warm milk and continue stirring until mixture thickens. Add seasoning and remove from heat to cool slightly.

- Beat egg yolks and add small amount of cream sauce to temper the yolks. Slowly add rest of yolks to sauce and mix well.

- Add sharp cheddar cheese. Return to heat, just enough to melt the cheese. Do not boil. Allow to cool.

- Beat egg whites until stiff and fold half into cheese sauce until incorporated. Gently fold in remaining egg whites.

- Carefully pour into dish and bake at 350°F, 40 to 45 minutes.

- Remove collar and serve immediately.

SERVES 6

GREEN BEANS WITH ZUCCHINI

1 pound fresh French-cut
 green beans

½ cup onion, minced

¼ cup butter or margarine

2 medium zucchinis, cut into
 ¼-inch slices

½ medium red bell pepper,
 sliced into strips

2 slices bacon, cooked
 and crumbled

- Wash beans, trim ends, and string if needed. Cut into 1½-inch pieces. Cook in boiling water for 15 to 20 minutes or until crisp and tender. Drain and refresh in ice water.

- Sauté onion in butter in large skillet about 3 minutes.

- Add zucchini and peppers; then continue to cook over medium-high heat for about 3 to 4 minutes, stirring constantly.

- Add green beans and cook until heated.

- This dish can be prepared ahead up to last step and finished before serving.

SERVES 6

RASPBERRY WALNUT SALAD

3 tablespoons rice wine vinegar

½ tablespoon sugar

⅓ cup walnut oil

1 tablespoon sour cream

1 tablespoon Dijon mustard

½ cup fresh, or frozen and
 defrosted, raspberries

2 heads fresh Bibb or butterhead
 lettuce, washed and torn

½ cup walnuts, coarsely chopped
 and toasted

- Whisk together vinegar, sugar, oil, sour cream, mustard, and about half the berries.

- Put lettuce in salad bowl or on plates and top with nuts and reserved berries.

- Drizzle with dressing and serve.

SERVES 6

THE "BEST" CREAM CHEESE POUND CAKE WITH PEACHES

8 ounces cream cheese

½ cup (1 stick) unsalted butter

2 sticks margarine

3 cups sugar

6 large eggs

3 cups sifted cake flour

¼ teaspoon salt

¼ teaspoon baking powder

1 teaspoon vanilla extract

1 teaspoon lemon extract

Vanilla ice cream

Fresh peaches, sliced and lightly
   sprinkled with sugar

- Bring cream cheese, butter, margarine, and eggs to room temperature and preheat oven to 325°F.

- Beat cream cheese, butter, and margarine until fluffy.

- Add sugar and beat well.

- While beating, add eggs, one at a time.

- Sift together salt, baking powder, flour, and add to creamed butter mixture a little at a time.

- Add vanilla and lemon extracts.

- Pour mixture into well-greased and floured Bundt pan. Bake for 1 hour and 15 minutes or until done.

- Let cake cool slightly in pan, before removing and cooling completely on wire rack. Serve slices of pound cake with scoop of vanilla ice cream and sugared peaches.

- Cake will keep several days in airtight container or can be frozen for later use.

SERVES 8

CLAIBORNE FARM

Cheese Wafers with Pecans

Grapefruit Salad with French Dressing

Crème de Volaille with Mushroom Sauce

Haricots Verts with Lemon Butter

Baked Kentucky Country Ham

Beaten Biscuits

Chocolate Macaroon Mousse

World-renowned Claiborne Farm gracefully upholds the tradition of the family farm passed down through generations. Since the mid-1970s Claiborne has been run by Seth W. Hancock, who followed his father, A.B. "Bull" Hancock Jr., and grandfather, A.B. Hancock Sr. Established about 1910, Claiborne has been the home of many mares and stallions owned by outside clients, as well as horses bred by the Hancock family. The farm spreads over more than 2,000 acres and includes several historic houses. Seth and his sisters, Clay and Dell, all live in homes on the property.

Claiborne's many distinctions include standing internationally important stallions, a practice begun by A.B. Hancock Sr. Under his son's leadership, Claiborne stallions led the sire list every year from 1955 to 1969 with key imports such as Princequillo and Nasrullah, as well as the Phipps family's farm-foaled Bold Ruler.

Seth Hancock's key acquisitions have included the multiple leading sires Danzig and Mr. Prospector, as well as Triple Crown winner Secretariat. By the end of the twentieth century, Claiborne sires had led the list twenty-eight years. At the same time, Hancock's breeding operation at Claiborne has produced many notable horses including international sires Caerleon and Nureyev while the Claiborne racing stable has won the Kentucky Derby and Belmont Stakes with Swale, the Travers with Forty Niner, and other important races.

A sentimental moment occurred late in the life of Mrs. A.B. Hancock Jr. when Yell won the 2003 Raven Run Stakes, earning Claiborne the coveted golden bowl and making the Hancocks the only racing family to earn a golden tray, pitcher, and the aforementioned bowl for accumulated Keeneland stakes victories.

CHEESE WAFERS WITH PECANS

1 cup unsalted butter, softened

2 cups all-purpose flour

½ pound grated sharp
   cheddar cheese

Dash or two of cayenne pepper

1 egg, slightly beaten

Whole pecans (for garnish)

Salt

- Preheat oven to 350°F.

- Combine butter, flour, cheese, and cayenne pepper with electric mixer on slow speed.

- Roll out on floured surface, ¼-inch thick, and cut rounds with small biscuit cutter.

- Place rounds on ungreased cookie sheet and brush with beaten egg. Place whole pecan on top for garnish.

- If you don't want pecan on top, prick top of wafer three times with a fork.

- Bake at 350°F for about 12 minutes. Sprinkle wafers with salt immediately after removing from oven.

MAKES APPROXIMATELY 5 DOZEN WAFERS

GRAPEFRUIT SALAD WITH FRENCH DRESSING

GRAPEFRUIT SALAD

3 grapefruits, peeled and
   sectioned

2 avocados, sliced

2 tablespoons lemon juice

Seeds from one pomegranate

6 ounces cream cheese, rolled
   into 6 to 8 small balls

1 head of red leaf lettuce

Paprika for garnish

FRENCH DRESSING

⅓ small onion, coarsely
   chopped

½ cup sugar

1 teaspoon salt

1 teaspoon paprika

1 teaspoon dry mustard

½ cup vegetable or canola oil

¼ cup apple cider vinegar

¼ cup freshly grated
   Parmesan cheese

- Slice grapefruit sections.

- Slice avocados and squeeze lemon over slices to prevent them from turning brown.

- Place grapefruit and avocado slices on bed of lettuce and sprinkle with pomegranate seeds.

- Top with small ball of cream cheese.

- For dressing, pulse onion in processor 3 or 4 times.

- Add next 6 dressing ingredients and pulse until mixture is emulsified.

- Add Parmesan cheese.

- Sprinkle grapefruit with paprika and drizzle with French dressing.

SERVES 6 TO 8

CRÈME DE VOLAILLE WITH MUSHROOM SAUCE

WHITE SAUCE

3 tablespoons unsalted butter

3 tablespoons flour

1 cup half & half

3 cups cooked chicken breasts, with ½ cup dark meat

¾ cup sliced fresh mushrooms, sautéed

2 tablespoons melted unsalted butter

3 eggs, beaten

2 teaspoons salt

1 teaspoon ground nutmeg

⅓ teaspoon red pepper

Fresh parsley for garnish

MUSHROOM SAUCE

3 tablespoons butter

¾ pound fresh mushrooms, thinly sliced

3 tablespoons flour

1 cup half & half

¼ teaspoon nutmeg

Salt and pepper to taste

- To make white sauce: On medium-low heat, melt butter in saucepan. Gradually add flour, whisking constantly. When blended, slowly add half & half. Continue whisking until sauce thickens. Keep warm until ready to use.

- In food processor, grind chicken along with mushrooms.

- In mixing bowl, combine chicken and mushroom mixture, white sauce, and remaining ingredients.

- Pour into greased 6-cup mold or loaf pan. Cover mold with foil. Place mold in pan with water 2 inches deep. Bake at 400°F for approximately 60 minutes or until "set."

- Loosen mold with knife. Invert onto platter.

- To make mushroom sauce, melt butter, add mushrooms, and sauté until soft. On low heat, whisk in flour, stirring for 1 minute.

- Gradually add half & half, nutmeg, and salt and pepper to taste, stirring until smooth and thickened.

- Spoon mushroom sauce on top of chicken loaf and garnish with fresh parsley.

SERVES 6 TO 8

HARICOTS VERTS WITH LEMON BUTTER

1½ pounds haricots verts

Salt

4 tablespoons (½ stick) unsalted butter

Juice of 1 lemon

Freshly ground black pepper

- Cook beans in salted boiling water for 4 minutes. Drain.

- Melt butter in small saucepan and let come to rich golden-brown color.

- Add lemon juice and beans and then toss. Season to taste with salt and pepper.

SERVES 6 TO 8

BAKED KENTUCKY COUNTRY HAM

1 country ham, preferably 18
  months old

½ cup whole cloves

1 cup brown sugar

1 cup cider vinegar

1½ gallons water

TOPPING

1 cup brown sugar

1 cup cornmeal

1 tablespoon ground cloves

1 teaspoon sugar

- Scrub ham with stiff brush to remove any mold. Immerse ham, skin side up, in cold water and soak overnight.

- Sprinkle ¼ cup of cloves in bottom of large roaster. Add ham, fat side up, and stick remaining cloves in fat. Add brown sugar, vinegar, and water to roaster; cover and bake at 375°F for 1 hour.

- Lower heat to 275°F and bake additional 20 minutes per pound.

- Cool slightly in roaster. Trim off fat.

- If desired, remove bone and tie ham securely with string. Refrigerate overnight.

- Remove string (if used) from ham. Combine topping ingredients thoroughly. Coat top of ham with topping and bake at 350°F until browned.

- Cool ham and slice thin pieces to serve on beaten biscuits.

BEATEN BISCUITS

7 cups soft wheat flour

3 tablespoons sugar

1 teaspoon salt

1 teaspoon baking powder

1 cup lard

1⅓ cups skim milk

- Combine flour, sugar, salt, and baking powder; work in lard with clean hands.

- Add most of milk to make stiff dough; add remaining milk as needed.

- Put dough in refrigerator for at least 2 hours to overnight.

- Allow dough to warm about 1 hour before dividing dough into fourths. Working with one-fourth at a time, cut into 1½-inch cubes.

- Place cubes in food processor and process for 2 minutes.

- On floured surface, roll out dough to ¼-inch thickness and cut with a 2-inch biscuit cutter.

- Place biscuits on ungreased cookie sheet; prick top of each biscuit with fork.

- Bake at 350°F for 25 minutes. Serve warm with slices of baked Kentucky country ham.

MAKES 6 DOZEN

CHOCOLATE MACAROON MOUSSE

2 dozen coconut macaroons
(medium, 3-inch diameter)

½ cup (plus 3 tablespoons)
cream sherry

1 pound semisweet chocolate

8 tablespoons water

1 cup plus 2 tablespoons sugar

8 eggs, separated

2 cups heavy cream

- Break macaroons into pieces and drizzle with ½ cup sherry; put aside and allow to soak for at least 30 minutes or longer.

- Melt chocolate, 8 tablespoons water, and 7 tablespoons sugar over very low heat, mixing well and stirring constantly.

- Remove mixture from stove and add 8 egg yolks one at a time, blending well. Set aside to let cool.

- Beat egg whites with 5 tablespoons sugar until stiff. Fold egg whites into cooled chocolate mixture. (You might need to transfer chocolate mixture into larger bowl before adding egg whites.)

- Whip cream, remaining 6 tablespoons sugar, and 3 tablespoons sherry to form sturdy peaks. Fold into chocolate mixture.

- Put layer of macaroons on bottom of dish then add layer of chocolate mousse mixture. Repeat layers, ending with chocolate mousse. Cover with plastic wrap and refrigerate overnight.

- When serving, cut into squares or spoon onto dessert plate. Top with dollop of additional whipped cream and garnish with grated chocolate curls.

SERVES 6 TO 8

KENTUCKY HORSE PARK

SUMMER TAILGATE

Cream of Pimento Soup

Shrimp Salad

Marinated Green Beans

Thai Marinated Chicken Strips

Frosted Cashew Drops

As an integral part of Kentucky history, heritage, and identity, horses add immeasurably to the quality of life in the Bluegrass. So it is only fitting that the Kentucky Horse Park honors the state's most recognized asset and the special relationship between horse and man. Framed by traditional white fences and harboring century-old trees, the Lexington park's more than 1,000 acres is home to internationally acclaimed museums, show rings, a cross-country course, a campground, the National Horse Center, the popular Parade of Breeds, and the Hall of Champions.

In addition, the horse park plays host each year to the Rolex Kentucky Three-Day Event, an Olympic-level "triathlon" for horses and riders. Winning the bid to host the 2010 Alltech FEI World Equestrian Games confirmed the park's place among the world's best equestrian sport facilities.

The Kentucky Horse Park Foundation, a not-for-profit organization, provides much of the crucial funding to enhance the park by purchasing horses, carriages, and life-sized bronzes of famous horses, as well as sponsoring world-class museum exhibitions and show facilities. *All the Queen's Horses* and *Imperial China*, which featured the excavated treasures of China's terra cotta warriors, illustrated the park's ability to attract and manage unique cultural opportunities for the park's visitors, which number nearly 1 million a year. *A Gift from the Desert*, an exhibit planned for 2010, promised to be the biggest exhibit to date.

The foundation also promotes several major fund-raisers each year such as the highly popular Southern Lights festival, a lighted tour of the park during the holiday season.

CREAM OF PIMENTO SOUP

1 (4-ounce) jar diced pimentos, drained

2 tablespoons unsalted butter

3½ tablespoons all-purpose flour

1 (14-ounce) can chicken broth

2 cups half & half

½ teaspoon salt

5 scallions, diced

¼ teaspoon Tabasco sauce

Fresh basil, chiffonaded for garnish

- Purée pimentos in blender and set aside.
- Melt butter in saucepan over low heat. Add flour, stirring constantly for one minute.
- Slowly add chicken broth and half & half.
- Cook mixture over medium heat until thick and bubbly.
- Stir in pimento purée, salt, scallions, and Tabasco sauce.
- Cook over low heat, stirring constantly until thoroughly heated.
- Chill. To serve, ladle into bowls or cups and top with basil chiffonade.

SERVES 8

SHRIMP SALAD

2–3 tablespoons kosher salt, plus 1 teaspoon

1 lemon, quartered

4 pounds large shrimp in the shell

2 cups mayonnaise

1 teaspoon Dijon mustard

2 tablespoons white wine vinegar

1 teaspoon freshly ground black pepper

6 tablespoons fresh dill, minced

1 cup red onion, minced

3 cups celery, minced

1 tablespoon lemon juice

- Bring 5 quarts of water, 1½ tablespoons salt, and quartered lemon to a boil in large saucepan. Add half the shrimp and reduce heat to medium.
- Cook uncovered for 3 minutes, or until shrimp is barely cooked through. Remove with slotted spoon to bowl of cool water.
- Bring water back to boil and repeat with remaining shrimp. Add remaining salt. Let shrimp cool; then peel and devein shrimp.
- In separate bowl, whisk mayonnaise, mustard, white wine vinegar, 1 teaspoon of salt, pepper, and dill. Combine with peeled shrimp.
- Add red onion, celery, lemon juice, and mix well. Check seasonings.
- Keep chilled until ready to serve.

SERVES 12

MARINATED GREEN BEANS

1 pound tender whole green beans

3 teaspoons chopped fresh flat-leaf parsley

1½ tablespoons red wine vinegar

1½ teaspoons Dijon mustard

⅓ cup olive oil

Freshly ground black pepper

1 small red onion, thinly sliced

- Cook green beans until barely tender.
- Drain and rinse beans with ice water; then dry.
- Whisk parsley, vinegar, mustard, olive oil, and pepper.
- Place beans in shallow dish and top with sliced red onions.
- Spoon vinaigrette over beans and onions.
- Serve hot or cold.

SERVES 8 TO 10

THAI MARINATED CHICKEN STRIPS

2 pounds medium-sized chicken breasts

MARINADE

1 cup crunchy peanut butter

¼ cup brown sugar

⅓ cup cilantro, chopped

½ cup soy sauce

½ cup chili sauce

8 scallions, chopped

1 tablespoon salt

3 tablespoons garlic, chopped

½ teaspoon freshly ground black pepper

¼ cup lime juice

15–20 small wooden skewers, soaked in water

- Thoroughly combine marinade ingredients.
- Trim chicken breasts into strips.
- Coat chicken with marinade and refrigerate for at least 3 hours or overnight.
- Thread chicken strips onto small prepared skewers.
- Grill for 6 minutes on each side.
- May be served hot or cold.

SERVES 8 TO 10

FROSTED CASHEW DROPS

½ cup butter

1 cup sugar

1 egg

½ teaspoon vanilla

2 cups flour

¾ tablespoon baking powder

¾ teaspoon salt

1 teaspoon cinnamon

¾ teaspoon nutmeg

⅓ cup sour cream

1 cup salted cashews, broken into pieces

FROSTING

3 tablespoons butter

2 cups powdered sugar

2 tablespoons milk

1 teaspoon vanilla

- Cream butter and sugar; then add egg and vanilla very slowly.
- Sift dry ingredients and add to creamed mixture a spoonful at a time, alternating with sour cream.
- Add cashew pieces.
- Roll into small balls and press flat with smooth-bottomed glass slightly greased in butter and dipped in sugar.
- Grease cookie sheet. Place cookies on sheet and bake at 350°F for about 6 to 8 minutes or until cookies have light-brown edges.
- While cookies are baking, make frosting. Heat butter, stirring constantly until slightly browned.
- Slowly beat in sugar, milk, and vanilla.
- Allow cookies to cool before pouring frosting over each cookie.

MAKES 4 DOZEN SMALL COOKIES

LANE'S END

FOURTH OF JULY PICNIC

Fried Banana Peppers

Barbecued Black Beans

Old-Fashioned Deviled Eggs

Onion Pie

Marinated Green Beans

Hamburgers Three Ways

Red, White, and Blue Cupcakes

Even with a background rooted in oil and other Texas businesses, William S. Farish has become very much a Kentuckian. Since 1980 Mr. and Mrs. Farish have called Versailles home.

Their 1½-story house at sprawling Lane's End Farm, originally known as Pleasant Lawn, was built in the 1820s. It resembles two houses built back-to-back, connected by recessed porticos with columns (twenty-one in all) and arches.

In addition to his many roles in Thoroughbred racing and breeding, Farish served as the U.S. ambassador to Great Britain early in the twenty-first century. Prior to that appointment, the Farishes hosted Queen Elizabeth II on her visit to the United States in the fall of 1984 and subsequently received her again on return visits. In 2007 the Farishes escorted Queen Elizabeth and Prince Philip to the Kentucky Derby.

Lane's End has become one of the industry's bulwarks in the stallion market and sales scene, as well as in racing. With Bill Farish Jr. taking on management responsibilities, too, Lane's End has stood such leading stallions as A.P. Indy and Kingmambo, topped Keeneland's prestigious yearling sales, and raced the homebred Horse of the Year Mineshaft and many other major stakes winners. William Farish has introduced many other sportsmen to the game, and in these and in other partnerships he has bred winners of each of the American Triple Crown races. Two of them, Kentucky Derby and Preakness winner Charismatic and Belmont winner A.P. Indy, were named Horse of the Year.

FRIED BANANA PEPPERS

2 sleeves Saltine crackers
(approximately 70 crackers)

All-purpose flour

4 eggs

½ cup beer

½ cup milk

2 (24-ounce) jars of pickled
banana peppers (6 peppers per
jar)

- Crush saltines in blender or food processor to very fine consistency and put in bowl.

- Put flour in second bowl.

- In third bowl, mix eggs, beer, and milk.

- Preheat oil, enough to allow peppers to float when frying, in deep fryer, to 450°F.

- Slice peppers and remove seeds. Dip pepper in egg wash; then roll in flour. Dip pepper again in egg wash, and this time roll in cracker crumbs.

- Carefully place in deep fryer and cook for 5 minutes or until browned. Remove and allow to drain on paper towel.

MAKES APPROXIMATELY 12 PEPPERS

BARBECUED BLACK BEANS

¼ pound of bacon
(4–5 pieces), cut up

1 cup red bell pepper, chopped

2 cups onion, chopped

2 teaspoons minced garlic

½ cup vegetable oil

4 (16-ounce) cans black beans,
rinsed and drained

½ tablespoon cumin

⅓ cup brown sugar

1 cup hickory-smoked
barbecue sauce

- Preheat oven to 350°F.

- Fry bacon pieces and remove from pan. Pour off some of grease. Add bell pepper, onion, garlic, and oil, and sauté until soft.

- In large ovenproof casserole dish, combine black beans, onion mixture, cumin, brown sugar, and barbecue sauce. Top with bacon.

- Place in oven and bake at 350°F for 45 minutes, until hot and bubbly.

SERVES 16

OLD-FASHIONED DEVILED EGGS

6 large eggs, hard-boiled, cooled
and peeled

3–4 tablespoons mayonnaise

3–4 tablespoons hot dog relish (a
mixture of yellow mustard and
sweet pickle relish)

Salt to taste

Parsley leaves, paprika, or thinly
slice green olives for garnish

- Slice eggs in half and carefully remove yolks. Put yolks in bowl.

- Mash yolks with fork so there are no lumps.

- Add mayonnaise and relish a little at a time until achieving a good consistency for stuffing.

- Add salt to taste and stuff eggs.

- Garnish, cover, and refrigerate or serve immediately.

- This recipe can be doubled or tripled, but for best results prepare in small batches.

YIELDS 12 DEVILED EGGS

ONION PIE

¾ stick unsalted butter, melted

1½ cups Club cracker crumbs

2 tablespoons butter, melted

2 cups sliced yellow onions

2 eggs, slightly beaten

¾ cup whole or 2% milk

¾ teaspoon each, salt and pepper

¼ cup grated cheddar cheese

Sprinkle of paprika

- Preheat oven to 350°F.

- Blend ¾-stick warm melted butter and cracker crumbs. Press this "crust" in pie pan, making sure to press crust up sides of pan. Set aside.

- Sauté onions in 2 tablespoons butter until limp. Put on top of crust.

- Combine eggs, milk, salt, and pepper and pour over onions. Cover with grated cheese and sprinkle with paprika.

- Bake uncovered at 350°F for 30 minutes or until brown. Makes a great side dish for grilled meat, chicken, or fish.

SERVES 8

MARINATED GREEN BEANS

3 pounds young, tender
green beans

MARINADE

3 teaspoons Beau Monde
Seasoning

3 tablespoons sour cream

2 teaspoons kosher salt

6 tablespoons tarragon
wine vinegar

1½ teaspoons cracked
black pepper

¾ cup olive oil

2 cloves garlic, finely chopped

2 tablespoons flat-leaf parsley,
finely chopped

¾ teaspoon Dijon mustard

- Blanch beans in boiling water 4 to 5 minutes. Remove and immerse in ice water bath. Drain and pat dry.

- In small bowl combine all marinade ingredients. Whisk until completely blended.

- Pour marinade over beans and refrigerate for at least 1 hour. Garnish with finely diced red onion or red bell peppers.

SERVES 12

HAMBURGERS THREE WAYS

6 pounds ground chuck beef

2 tablespoons kosher salt

2 teaspoons black pepper

MUSHROOM, ONION, AND FONTINA CHEESE

½ pound mushrooms, chopped

1 onion, diced

4 ounces Fontina cheese, grated

BLUE CHEESE AND BACON

6 ounces Saga blue cheese, crumbled

2 tablespoons flat-leaf parsley, chopped

5 slices cooked bacon, crumbled

BASIL, MOZZARELLA, AND DICED TOMATOES

½–1 cup basil, chopped

6 ounces mozzarella, shredded

1 cup diced fresh summer tomatoes, seeded, chopped, and drained

- Using your hands, combine ground hamburger with salt and pepper. Form into thin patties.

- For mushroom, onion, and fontina cheese filling, sauté mushrooms and onions in small amount of butter; allow to cool slightly.

- Mix mushrooms and onions with fontina cheese. Use generous teaspoon of mixture to stuff each burger.

- For blue cheese and bacon filling, mix cheese, bacon, and parsley. Use generous teaspoon of mixture to stuff each burger.

- For basil, mozzarella, and diced tomato filling, mix all ingredients well. Use generous teaspoon to stuff each burger.

- After placing one of the fillings on one side of a patty, place a second patty on top and press to seal side of burger. Be careful not to press too hard and pop filling out of burger.

- Grill until done and cheeses have melted.

- We also suggest a tray of lettuces, sliced summer yellow and red heirloom tomatoes, and sliced Vidalia and Bermuda onions for hamburgers. On the opposite page are two special mayonnaise recipes to spread on hamburger buns.

YIELDS 12

DIXIELAND BAND

BASIL MAYONNAISE

1 cup mayonnaise

½ cup basil, chopped fine

¼ cup chopped chives

1 teaspoon lemon juice

1 teaspoon Dijon mustard

- Combine ingredients and refrigerate until ready to use on hamburgers.

CHIPOTLE MAYONNAISE

1 cup mayonnaise

⅛ teaspoon cumin,
   or more to taste

½ cup sour cream

2 small cloves garlic, minced

2 tablespoons fresh lime juice

2 chipotle chiles in adobo sauce

- Mix all ingredients well and refrigerate until ready to use on hamburgers.

RED, WHITE, AND BLUE CUPCAKES

1 box classic white cake mix

¾ cup vegetable oil

4 large eggs

16 ounces frozen strawberries,
   thawed and sliced

1 cup finely chopped nuts

ICING

1 (8-ounce) package cream cheese

1½–2 cups powdered sugar

¼ cup unsalted butter

1½ teaspoon vanilla

Blueberries, raspberries, or
   strawberries for garnish

- In large mixing bowl, combine cake mix and oil. While electric mixer is running, add eggs one at a time, being sure to incorporate well after each addition.

- Add strawberries and nuts. Pour into muffin tins lined with cupcake liners.

- Bake according to box instructions.

- Combine cream cheese and butter in mixing bowl. Add powdered sugar and vanilla and beat well.

- Cover cooled cupcakes with icing and top each with a blueberry, red raspberry, or sliced strawberry half.

YIELDS APPROXIMATELY 24 CUPCAKES

MIDDLEBROOK FARM

SUMMER SUPPER ON THE TERRACE

Guacamole El Nopalito

Jalapeño Cornbread

Arugula Salad with Shaved Parmesan

Baked Rice

Limed Sugar Snaps

Baked Sea Bass in Tomatillo Sauce

White Flan

Helen Alexander grew up deeply involved with horses. Her grandfather Robert Kleberg Jr. headed the racing and breeding operation of the renowned King Ranch in Texas and raised Triple Crown winner Assault and another Kentucky Derby winner, Middleground. Alexander managed the Kentucky division of King Ranch for a number of years before purchasing her own farm, Middlebrook, in 1985.

Like other properties in the Bluegrass, the land has its unique history. The house on Middlebrook dates from about 1835, when the property was known as the A.S. Drake farm. Drake was president of Transylvania University in Lexington, the first college west of the Allegheny Mountains. After his retirement from that institution, Drake continued as an educator, running Prospect Academy on the farm. Prospect Academy specialized in classical studies. The farm is also the site of a prehistoric Indian mound.

Middlebrook today covers 350 acres, on which Alexander primarily raises horses for herself and her mother and sisters. Distinguished runners produced at Middlebrook include Arch, Bertolini, and Exchange Rate (a $1.4 million sale yearling), each a prominent stallion in the early twenty-first century. Also, Cee's Tizzy, the sire of 2000 Horse of the Year and two-time Breeders' Cup Classic winner Tiznow, was raised at Middlebrook.

One of the mainstays of Alexander's breeding operation was Broodmare of the Year Courtly Dee, who produced 1983 champion two-year-old filly Althea, later a distinguished broodmare herself. Among Althea's daughters that also became outstanding broodmares is Arch's dam, Aurora.

GUACAMOLE EL NOPALITO

4 very ripe medium avocados
   (preferably Hass), peeled
   and pitted

1 teaspoon salt

1 cup minced tomato, drained

½ cup minced red onion

Juice of 1 lime

½ teaspoon red pepper flakes

¼ cup fresh cilantro, chopped
   (optional)

Corn tortilla chips,
   as accompaniment

- Place avocado in bowl; add salt, mashing with fork.

- Stir in remaining ingredients.

- Serve with corn tortilla chips.

SERVES 8

JALAPEÑO CORNBREAD

Vegetable cooking spray

½ cup olive oil

1½ cups self-rising cornmeal

1 (8.5-ounce) can cream-style corn

¼ cup self-rising flour

2–3 jalapeño peppers, chopped
   (1–3 tablespoons canned
   and chopped)

8 ounces low-fat sour cream

2 eggs beaten

1 small to medium Vidalia onion,
   chopped

1 cup sharp cheddar cheese,
   shredded

- Preheat oven to 350°F.

- Spray 9x13-inch baking pan with cooking spray. Place pan in oven to warm.

- Mix all ingredients except cheese in large bowl.

- Pour batter into warm, prepared pan and top with cheese.

- Bake for approximately 30 to 40 minutes. Watch carefully and remove when brown on top.

SERVES 8

ARUGULA SALAD WITH SHAVED PARMESAN

2 (5-ounce) containers of arugula

½ cup shaved Parmigiano-
Reggiano cheese

⅓ cup white wine vinegar

½ teaspoon Dijon mustard

1 cup olive oil

½ teaspoon minced fresh garlic

¾ teaspoon kosher salt

½ teaspoon freshly ground
black pepper

- In a bowl, whisk together vinegar, mustard, garlic, salt, and pepper.
  Slowly add the olive oil until the vinaigrette is emulsified.

- Toss the greens with dressing and then add shaved
  Parmigiano-Reggiano.

SERVES 8

BAKED RICE

2 cups uncooked rice

2½ cups chicken broth

½ teaspoon salt or to taste

2 tablespoons unsalted butter

1½ tablespoons flat-leaf parsley,
finely chopped, optional

1½ tablespoons onion, finely
chopped, optional

1½ tablespoons celery, finely
chopped, optional

- Preheat oven to 350°F.

- Combine all ingredients, including optional ingredients if desired,
  and put in 5x9-inch loaf pan or 2-quart round casserole dish. Cover
  with aluminum foil and seal snugly.

- Bake at 350°F for 1 hour and 15 minutes or until rice is tender.
  (To decrease cooking time, use boiling chicken broth.)

SERVES 8

LIMED SUGAR SNAPS

1½–2 pounds sugar snap peas

Salt for water

2 tablespoons butter

1 tablespoon lime juice

- Wash and remove ends and any strings on peas.

- Blanch peas in boiling salted water for 3 to 5 minutes. Drain and cover with ice. After cooled, place peas on paper towels to dry.

- Melt 2 tablespoons butter in pan. Add peas to pan and salt and pepper to taste. Sauté peas until warm. Pour lime juice over peas and serve immediately.

SERVES 8

BAKED SEA BASS IN TOMATILLO SAUCE

8 (4-ounce) fillets or 1 large piece of sea bass

½ cup sour cream

Chopped cilantro for garnish

TOMATILLO SAUCE

16 small tomatillos

4 cups water

4 teaspoons oil

½ onion, chopped

2 serrano chiles, minced

2 cloves garlic, minced

2 teaspoons salt

4 teaspoons lime juice

- Remove husks and wash tomatillos under running water. Place tomatillos in 4 cups water in a saucepan and bring to boil. Simmer until tender, approximately 10 minutes.

- Using blender or food processor, purée tomatillos in the liquid and then set aside.

- Sauté onion, chiles, and garlic in oil until tender, 1 to 2 minutes. Stir in tomatillo mixture, bring to simmer, and cook until it thickens slightly, about 5 minutes. Season with salt and lime juice.

- Put sea bass fillets in baking dish and pour tomatillo sauce over fish. Bake at 375°F until fish flakes easily, about 30 minutes.

- Before serving, spoon a bit of sour cream over fish and sprinkle with cilantro.

- For spicier fish use 3 or 4 serrano chiles.

SERVES 8

WHITE FLAN

12 egg whites

⅛ teaspoon salt

½ teaspoon cream of tartar

¾–1 cup sugar (6–8 ounces)

½ teaspoon vanilla

1½ teaspoons vanilla extract

½ teaspoon almond extract

CARAMEL

½ teaspoon salt

1½ cups sugar (12 ounces)

TOPPING

1 cup heavy cream

Pinch of salt

1 tablespoon powdered sugar

½ teaspoon vanilla extract

¼ teaspoon almond extract

1 cup toasted blanched almond
   halves for garnish

- Preheat oven to 350°F.

- Place ingredients for caramel in heavy saucepan over medium heat. Swirl pan constantly until sugar melts and caramelizes, turning a light golden-brown.

- Pour caramel into 2-quart ring mold or Bundt pan and tilt so caramel covers bottom and sides. Set aside.

- Place egg whites in large bowl; add salt and cream of tartar, beating until egg whites form stiff peaks. Fold in sugar and add extracts. Pour mixture into caramel-coated mold (caramel should be hard by this time).

- Set mold in larger pan and pour 1 inch of boiling water in pan. Place in oven and bake for 45 to 60 minutes. Do not remove mold from oven immediately; instead, turn off oven and leave mold in oven with door open for 10 minutes before taking it out. Be careful to put mold in a spot where there are no drafts or extreme temperature changes.

- When mold has cooled to room temperature (approximately 20 minutes), unmold flan onto platter and cover with caramel sauce. To remove any caramel that sticks to mold, place 1 cup water in mold and hold mold over hot burner on the stove, stirring until caramel is loosened; let mold cool a little and pour caramel over flan.

- To prepare topping, beat cream with pinch of salt. When it begins to thicken, add sugar and extracts. Beat until stiff. Spoon dollops of cream onto flan and garnish with almond halves.

SERVES 8

 104   BLUEGRASS WINNERS

OVERBROOK FARM

PICNIC AT THE COTTAGE

Chilled Carrot Apple Soup with Ginger

Chicken Salad with Sliced Avocado and Tomatoes

Fresh Blueberry Muffins

Strawberry and Rhubarb Cobbler

Lexington businessman W.T. Young and his wife, Lucy, demonstrated their love of the land and history as they developed Overbrook Farm. The nineteenth-century home of a gristmill operator along East Hickman Creek was restored and remodeled on the original tract of 110 acres that launched Overbrook in 1972. Subsequently, some thirty other parcels were added as Young established a picturesque property of rolling meadows, wooded areas, and handsome Federal-style buildings and barns.

In the early 1980s Young made some astute equine purchases upon which generations of excellence would be built. The mare Terlingua became the dam of Overbrook's great stallion Storm Cat, and the mare Cinegita was to be the granddam of champion Flanders, who in turn foaled champion Surfside.

In 1994 Overbrook won its first classic races when a partnership-owned Tabasco Cat, a son of Storm Cat, took both the Preakness and Belmont stakes. He was followed by partnership-owned Timber Country, who won the Preakness the next year, and then by Kentucky Derby winner Grindstone and Belmont Stakes winner Editor's Note in 1996.

Meanwhile, Storm Cat had begun collecting multiple titles as America's leading sire overall and leading sire of two-year-olds. With more than 150 stakes winners and earners of more than $100 million, he helped Overbrook join the ranks of Kentucky's most accomplished farms. Overbrook's own distinguished runners include Breeders' Cup Classic winner Cat Thief, Kentucky Oaks winner Seaside Attraction, and champions Golden Attraction and Boston Harbor.

Since the death of Young in 2004, his son, William T. Young Jr., and his son, Christopher Young, have continued to operate Overbrook. Mr. Young's daughter, Lucy Young Hamilton, also is involved.

CHILLED CARROT APPLE SOUP WITH GINGER

1 large onion, chopped

1 tablespoon olive oil

3 cups chicken broth

1½ cups water

1½ pounds of carrots,
  peeled and sliced

1½ teaspoons salt

1 tart apple, peeled, cored,
  and chopped

1 tablespoon chopped
  fresh ginger

¼ cup fresh orange juice

Sour cream and snipped
  chives for garnish

- Sauté onion in olive oil until soft (do not brown) in a 3–4-quart stockpot.

- Add all remaining ingredients except orange juice and bring to boil. Turn heat down, partially cover, and simmer until vegetables are very tender, about 30 minutes. Cool slightly.

- Purée soup in food processor or blender in small batches so it does not splatter.

- Pour into large container and add orange juice, mixing well. Chill and adjust salt. Chilled soup often needs more salt.

- To serve: Ladle soup into bowls; top with a dollop of sour cream and snipped chives.

MAKES 6 TO 8 CUPS

CHICKEN SALAD WITH SLICED AVOCADO AND TOMATOES

2 pounds boneless chicken breast,
  cooked and chopped into
  ½-inch dice-shaped pieces

1 cup (3 stalks) celery, chopped
  into ½-inch dice-shaped pieces

3 tablespoons capers

½ cup mayonnaise

Salt and pepper to taste

Lettuce to line plates

Tomato and avocado slices
  to garnish plates

Light vinaigrette to taste

- Combine chicken, celery, capers, and mayonnaise. Add salt and pepper to taste.

- Serve on Bibb or Boston lettuce with tomato and avocado slices.

- Drizzle light amount of vinaigrette over tomato and avocado. (This salad also can be made with fresh lobster.)

SERVES 4 TO 6

FRESH BLUEBERRY MUFFINS

2½ cups all-purpose flour

¾ cup sugar

½ teaspoon nutmeg

1 tablespoon baking powder

Dash of salt

6 tablespoons unsalted butter

2 eggs, slightly beaten

1 cup milk

1 teaspoon vanilla

1–1½ cups fresh blueberries

- Preheat oven to 350°F.

- In large mixing bowl, combine flour, sugar, nutmeg, baking powder, and salt.

- Slice butter into ½-inch pieces and cut in to flour mixture using pastry blender, 2 knives, or fingertips. In small bowl, combine eggs with milk and vanilla.

- When mixture resembles oatmeal, add egg and milk mixture. Mix lightly with spoon until batter is just moistened. Do not use electric mixer!

- Gently stir in blueberries.

- Fill greased and floured muffin cups ¾ full and bake at 350°F for about 30 minutes or until golden-brown and baked through.

MAKES APPROXIMATELY 16 MEDIUM-SIZED MUFFINS

STRAWBERRY AND RHUBARB COBBLER

1⅓–1⅔ cups sugar

⅓ cup all-purpose flour

1 teaspoon cinnamon

¾ teaspoon nutmeg

4 cups fresh rhubarb, cut in ½-inch pieces, or 1 cup sliced strawberries and 3 cups rhubarb, cut in ½-inch pieces

2 tablespoons unsalted butter

1 (9-inch) ready-made pie crust (or made from scratch)

- Preheat oven to 425°F.

- Combine sugar, flour, cinnamon, and nutmeg.

- Turn half of rhubarb and strawberries into a pie pan or other baking dish and sprinkle with half the sugar-flour mixture.

- Repeat with remaining rhubarb, strawberry, and sugar-flour mixture.

- Dot with butter.

- Cut pie crust into strips and weave lattice top over rhubarb mixture. Start with longest pastry strips in center and work your way out, with shorter strips on outside. Fold half the strips in half for the shorter strips. Lay strips going other way starting at center as well and working to sides. Repeat, alternating directions until pie is covered.

- Crimp edges of crust and bake 40 to 50 minutes until crust is golden-brown and juice begins to bubble through spaces in crust. (Sometimes juice bubbles over, so place cookie sheet or foil on rack beneath pie to catch juices.)

SERVES 6 TO 8

STOCKPLACE

Marinated Cucumber Sandwiches

Gorgonzola Pasta

BLT Salad with Balsamic Vinaigrette

Grilled Bone-In Beef Rib Eye Steaks with Henry Bain Sauce

Sautéed Squash and Zucchini

Blueberry Pie

Stockplace was originally named VanMeter Stockplace for the men who settled it in Clark County, Kentucky, in the late 1700s. These ancestors of Dr. Thomas F. VanMeter, an equine veterinarian, were farmers and pre-eminent breeders of short-horn cattle. Today, Stockplace, which comprises more than nine hundred acres of farmland in Fayette and Clark counties, is a commercial Thoroughbred breeding operation. VanMeter and his wife, Gay, live on Stockplace raising Thoroughbreds and children and entertaining many friends and clients. Mrs. VanMeter is the daughter of Mr. and Mrs. Louis Lee Haggin III. Louis Haggin is a trustee of Keeneland and descendant of James Ben Ali Haggin of Elmendorf Farm.

VanMeter is also a partner in Eaton Sales, a Thoroughbred bloodstock agency that consigns horses to the major sales at Keeneland and Fasig-Tipton.

Outstanding runners bred and/or owned by VanMeter in recent years include 2005 Kentucky Oaks winner Summerly, Victory U.S.A., Be Gentle, Mackie, Brahms, and Mr. John.

MARINATED CUCUMBER SANDWICHES

2 medium-sized cucumbers

1 cup white vinegar

4 tablespoons water

2 tablespoons sugar

1 teaspoon dill weed

½ teaspoon dill seed

Salt to taste

Approximately 3 tablespoons mayonnaise

Lemon juice to taste

1½ loaves of very thin white sandwich bread or 2 loaves of party rye

Paprika to garnish

- Slice cucumbers and layer in bowl, sprinkling salt on each layer. Cover cucumbers with plate or other top and put weight on top to compact cucumbers.

- Let cucumbers sit for 1 to 2 hours. While cucumbers are resting in salt, combine vinegar and next five ingredients in a jar. Shake brine well and set aside.

- Remove cucumbers from bowl, rinse, and pat dry.

- Place cucumbers in another bowl and pour brine over top, making sure liquid surrounds all cucumbers. Soak cucumbers in brine at least 1 hour.

- Mix mayonnaise with a few drops of lemon juice.

- With 2-inch biscuit cutter, cut bread in rounds. Spread mayonnaise on one side of bread.

- Remove enough cucumbers from brine to construct sandwiches. Gently pat cucumbers with paper towel to dry. Place 1 cucumber slice on top of each bread circle and sprinkle with paprika.

- Serve immediately or cover and keep chilled until ready to serve.

MAKES 24 SANDWICHES

GORGONZOLA PASTA

2 tablespoons salted butter

5 scallions, finely chopped

1 tablespoon plus 2 teaspoons chopped fresh thyme or 1½ teaspoons dried thyme leaves

2 cups heavy cream

½ pound gorgonzola cheese, crumbled

Salt and pepper to taste

1½ pounds fusilli (or bow tie or penne) pasta, cooked

½ cup Parmesan cheese, freshly grated

- Melt butter and add scallions to cook until translucent. Stir in thyme and add cream and gorgonzola. Season with salt and pepper. Continue stirring until cheese is melted and well incorporated.

- Pour sauce over pasta and sprinkle with Parmesan. Serve immediately.

SERVES 6

BLT SALAD WITH BALSAMIC VINAIGRETTE

2 hearts of Romaine lettuce, coarsely chopped

1 small head iceberg lettuce, coarsely chopped

1½ cups tomatoes, seeded and diced

6 slices bacon, cooked and crumbled

3 hardboiled eggs, chopped

- Combine lettuces in a large bowl.

- Top with tomatoes, bacon, and eggs. Drizzle balsamic vinaigrette over top and toss.

SERVES 6 TO 8

BALSAMIC VINAIGRETTE

1 cup good-quality olive oil

1 teaspoon lemon juice

½ cup aged balsamic vinegar

1 tablespoon chopped fresh basil

1 teaspoon Dijon mustard

1 teaspoon garlic salt

1 teaspoon freshly ground black pepper

- Combine all ingredients in mason jar and shake well and vigorously.

MAKES 2 CUPS

GRILLED BONE-IN BEEF RIB EYE STEAKS WITH HENRY BAIN SAUCE

1 bone-in beef rib eye steak per person

HENRY BAIN SAUCE:

1 (14-ounce) bottle ketchup

1 (10-ounce) bottle Worcestershire sauce

1 (12-ounce) bottle chili sauce

1 (8-ounce) jar Major Grey's chutney

1 (10-ounce) bottle A.1. Steak Sauce

2 tablespoons Tabasco sauce

- Select steaks to serve 1 per person and grill accordingly.

- Combine all sauce ingredients, mixing well, and pour into bottles. Sauce will keep for months in the refrigerator.

- Serve grilled steaks with Henry Bain sauce.

MAKES APPROXIMATELY 6¾ CUPS HENRY BAIN SAUCE

SAUTÉED SQUASH AND ZUCCHINI

2 tablespoons of butter

2 tablespoons of olive oil

1 medium onion, sliced thin

2 medium zucchini, cut in diagonal ¼-inch pieces

2 medium yellow squash, cut in diagonal ¼-inch pieces

Kosher salt and freshly ground black pepper, to taste

½ cup fresh basil, chiffonaded

- In medium cast-iron skillet, heat olive oil and butter to medium-high heat. Add onions and sauté until tender and slightly caramelized, 10 to 15 minutes.

- Add zucchini and yellow squash, adding more olive oil if necessary. Cook until squashes are still crunchy (5 to 8 minutes). Salt and pepper to taste. Garnish with basil strips.

SERVES 6

BLUEBERRY PIE

Pie crust for top and bottom

1½ cups sugar

3 tablespoons cornstarch

½ teaspoon salt

3 tablespoons tapioca, quick cooking

1 teaspoon lemon zest, finely grated

6½ cups fresh blueberries

- Preheat oven to 425°F. Preheat baking sheet.

- Combine all pie filling ingredients except blueberries. Gently fold in blueberries.

- Spoon filling into deep-dish pie pan lined with 1 unbaked pie crust. Cover mixture with second pie crust. Press edges together to seal and cut 3 to 4 steam vents in top.

- Bake pie on heated baking sheet for 30 minutes; reduce temperature to 375°F and continue baking for about 40 minutes, until pie crust is golden and filling is bubbling. Serve warm with vanilla ice cream.

SERVES 6 TO 8

THREE CHIMNEYS FARM

Corn and Red Pepper Soup

Lamb and Arugula Salad with Honey-Mint Vinaigrette

Perciatelli with Garden Tomatoes, Pancetta, and Red Pepper

Almond Cake with Strawberries

Politics dominated the professional life of the statesman Henry Clay, but he also bred racehorses. Robert Clay, one of his many descendants, has limited his political experience more or less to the workings of the Thoroughbred industry while also excelling as a businessman and horseman. Among the touches on his Three Chimneys Farm that resonate both of history and a modern approach is a timbered structure that serves as a stallion barn. It looks very old and converted but in fact was designed and built specifically for the horses.

Robert and Blythe Clay have built Three Chimneys from a hundred-acre farm offering boarding in a converted tobacco barn into a multi-division operation well known for the quality of its select stallion band. By 1984 Clay was ready to make a bold step when he worked with Jim and Sally Hill and Karen and Mickey Taylor in recruiting Slew o' Gold for the farm. That connection soon found the champion's sire, Triple Crown winner Seattle Slew, joining the son at Three Chimneys and becoming a popular tourist attraction.

In acquiring stallions for his farm, Clay has dealt with a variety of personalities, including the Aga Khan, from whom he secured the English Derby winner Shahrastani, and retired auto dealer Roy Chapman, who owned Smarty Jones. When Smarty Jones became a public hero by winning the Kentucky Derby and Preakness in 2004, many farms approached Roy and Pat Chapman. The couple selected Three Chimneys, in part because they wanted the public to be able to visit the champion.

CORN AND RED PEPPER SOUP

6 fresh ears of corn

2 tablespoons olive oil

1 medium onion, finely chopped

1 celery stalk, finely chopped

1 red bell pepper, seeded and finely chopped

2 cloves garlic, crushed

3 medium potatoes, peeled and chopped

2 cups chicken broth

4 cups water

- Cut corn kernels from cobs. Reserve cobs.

- Heat olive oil in large saucepan over medium heat. Cook onion, celery, red pepper, and garlic for 5 minutes, until soft.

- Add corn kernels and potatoes and cook 2 minutes.

- Add broth, reserved cobs, and 4 cups of water. Bring to a boil. Reduce temperature to medium-low and simmer for 30 minutes. Potatoes need to be tender.

- Discard cobs and purée soup in a blender or food processor. Strain soup through fine sieve back into saucepan. Season with salt and pepper to taste.

SERVES 6

LAMB AND ARUGULA SALAD WITH HONEY-MINT VINAIGRETTE

LAMB

¼ teaspoon oregano

¼ cup olive oil

1 tablespoon sherry vinegar

1 clove garlic, crushed

1 teaspoon Angostura bitters

¾ teaspoon salt

½ teaspoon freshly ground pepper

½ teaspoon cumin

4 lamb loins

ARUGULA SALAD

1 pound arugula, washed and dried

1 head radicchio, torn into small pieces

36 grapes, halved

2 tablespoons pine nuts, toasted

½ cup fresh Parmesan cheese, shaved

HONEY-MINT VINAIGRETTE

2 tablespoons sherry vinegar

1 tablespoon fresh mint, chopped

1½ teaspoons fresh lemon juice

Salt and freshly ground black pepper to taste

1½ teaspoons Dijon mustard

1 tablespoon honey

¾ cup olive or canola oil

- Combine all marinade ingredients in large resealable plastic bag. Add lamb loins. Marinate in refrigerator 6 to 12 hours.

- Bring lamb to room temperature. Discard marinade. Preheat oven to 350°F.

- Heat large skillet over high heat with a little oil until smoking. Add lamb and sear on all sides, approximately 3 minutes.

- Place seared lamb loins on sheet pan and roast in oven for 20 minutes.

- Remove from oven and let lamb return to room temperature. Cut lamb into ¼-inch–to–½-inch thick slices.

- Toss arugula and radicchio together. Arrange lamb slices over arugula and radicchio. Top with grape halves, pine nuts, and Parmesan.

- In medium bowl, combine all vinaigrette ingredients but oil. Slowly whisk in oil. Drizzle over prepared salad.

SERVES 6

PERCIATELLI WITH GARDEN TOMATOES, PANCETTA, AND RED PEPPER

1 pound perciatelli or bucatini pasta

1 tablespoon olive oil

4 ounces thinly sliced pancetta, finely chopped

1 teaspoon fresh garlic, minced

¼ teaspoon red pepper flakes

2 cups fresh tomatoes, peeled, seeded, and coarsely chopped

½ cup fresh Parmesan cheese, grated

¼ cup Pecorino Romano cheese, grated

- Bring 4 quarts of well-salted water to a boil. Cook pasta al dente (tender but firm to the bite). Drain and allow to cool, reserving ½ cup of pasta water.

- In large frying pan, heat oil over medium heat. Add pancetta, and cook until it begins to crisp. Add garlic and red pepper flakes. Cook 2 minutes, reducing heat if necessary.

- Add tomatoes and cook 2 minutes. Add pasta and pasta water. Cook until well heated.

- Top with cheeses and serve.

SERVES 6

ALMOND CAKE WITH STRAWBERRIES

1 pound strawberries, hulled and quartered

⅓ cup sugar

CAKE

1¼ cups sugar

1 (7-ounce) package marzipan or almond paste

1 cup unsalted butter, softened

6 eggs

1 cup all-purpose flour

1 teaspoon baking powder

Confectioner's sugar to dust

Vanilla ice cream

- Place strawberries in bowl and mix with ⅓ cup sugar; let stand.

- Preheat oven to 325°F. Grease and line bottom of 10-inch springform pan with parchment paper.

- Combine 1¼ cups sugar and marzipan in food processor. Add butter and process until mixture is light and fluffy.

- Add eggs one at a time, blending after each addition.

- Add flour and baking powder. Mix well.

- Spread batter into pan and cover pan with foil. Bake for 30 to 35 minutes, or until toothpick comes out clean.

- Remove cake from oven and cool in pan for 10 minutes. Carefully remove cake from springform pan. Dust cake with confectioner's sugar. Serve slices of cake with strawberries and vanilla ice cream.

SERVES 6

VINERY

Spinach Artichoke Asiago Spread

Limestone Bibb Lettuce with Goat Cheese, Pecans, and Sorghum Vinaigrette

Marinated and Grilled Beef Tenderloin

Horseradish Aspic

Balsamic Glazed Asparagus

Vinery Potatoes

Warm Chocolate Cakes with Bourbon Crème Anglaise

Dr. Tom Simon's Lexington division of Vinery is part of an international enterprise that also has divisions in Florida and in Australia. Covering 440 acres, the Lexington headquarters is a full-service operation that includes a stallion division; facilities for broodmares, weanlings, and yearlings; and provisions for breaking and training. The training and rehab complex for farm horses and client horses has a half-mile training track, an Aquatred exercise machine, and a Polytrack walking area and shed row. The ambience of the Bluegrass region is fulfilled as well by the presence of a handsome home and professionally designed gardens.

Simon's vision for Vinery was certified early on by the success of the first draft of young stallions he acquired. The remarkable More Than Ready stood both in North America and in Australia and immediately made an impact on both continents. Vinery stood Red Ransom before moving him to Sheikh Mohammed bin Rashid al Maktoum's Dalham Hall Stud in England. Red Ransom sired Electrocutionist, 2006 winner of the world's richest race, the $6-million Dubai World Cup. Later additions to Vinery promise to continue the successful pattern, with horses such as Yonaguska, Purge, Limehouse, Pure Prize, Silver Train, and Posse bringing to the stud barn exceptional racing performances and bloodlines.

SPINACH ARTICHOKE ASIAGO SPREAD

1 (16-ounce) package frozen chopped spinach

1 (14-ounce) package frozen artichoke hearts

1 (8-ounce) package cream cheese, softened

1 cup mayonnaise

1 cup finely shredded Asiago cheese

4 cloves garlic, minced

- Preheat oven to 375°F.

- Thaw spinach and artichoke hearts. Squeeze excess moisture from spinach and coarsely chop artichoke hearts.

- Combine all ingredients in medium bowl and blend well.

- Place mixture in buttered casserole dish and bake at 375°F for 25 to 30 minutes or until browned on top.

- Serve warm with baguette slices or crackers. Also good as a vegetable dip.

SERVES 10 TO 12

LIMESTONE BIBB LETTUCE
WITH GOAT CHEESE, PECANS, AND SORGHUM VINAIGRETTE

3–4 heads limestone Bibb lettuce

8 ounces goat cheese, broken into pieces

8 ounces toasted pecans, chopped

SORGHUM VINAIGRETTE

1 tablespoon Kentucky sorghum molasses, unsulphured

1 tablespoon grainy Dijon mustard

¼ cup apple cider vinegar, preferably unfiltered

¾ cup extra virgin olive oil

Sea salt and cracked black pepper to taste.

- Wash and dry lettuce well and tear into quarters. Place lettuce on a large, deep platter and scatter with goat cheese pieces. Sprinkle with pecans and dress with vinaigrette.

- Whisk together sorghum, mustard, and vinegar. Add olive oil in a slow, steady stream while continuing to whisk.

- Add salt and pepper. Will keep covered and unrefrigerated for several days.

SERVES 8 TO 10

MARINATED AND GRILLED BEEF TENDERLOIN

1 (6–8 pound) beef tenderloin, well trimmed

MARINADE

1 cup A.1. Steak Sauce

¼ cup Dijon mustard

½ cup dry red wine

½ cup extra virgin olive oil

1 tablespoon coarsely ground black pepper

- Combine all marinade ingredients and pour over tenderloin. Place beef in refrigerator and marinate for at least 2 hours, turning periodically.

- Remove tenderloin from refrigerator 1 hour before cooking. Remove meat from marinade and place on hot grill, turning every 2 to 3 minutes to mark over entire surface. May baste with reserved marinade if desired.

- After 15 minutes, check meat's internal temperature with instant-read meat thermometer (120°F for rare, 140°F for medium-rare).

- Remove tenderloin from grill and allow to sit, covered in foil, for 15 minutes before slicing.

SERVES 8 TO 10

HORSERADISH ASPIC

2 (1-ounce) packages unflavored gelatin

½ cup boiling water

4–8 ounces prepared horseradish

2 cups heavy cream, whipped

2 tablespoons flat-leaf parsley, finely chopped

- Coat a 4-cup mold with cooking spray.

- Dissolve gelatin in boiling water and let cool.

- Fold horseradish into whipped cream.

- Fold in chopped parsley and dissolved gelatin, thoroughly blending mixture. Pour into mold and refrigerate until set.

- To unmold, loosen aspic around the edges with a table knife and invert over serving platter. It should slip out easily. If not, dip bottom of mold briefly in hot water and try again.

SERVES 8 TO 10

BALSAMIC GLAZED ASPARAGUS

4 pounds fresh asparagus

1 cup balsamic vinegar

½ cup extra virgin olive oil

1 tablespoon coarse sea salt

1 tablespoon freshly
ground black pepper

- Preheat oven to 450°F.

- Trim asparagus and spread evenly over 2 sheet pans.

- In heavy saucepan, over medium-low heat, simmer vinegar until reduced by half.

- Drizzle vinegar over asparagus and sprinkle with salt and pepper. Drizzle with olive oil, rolling to coat evenly.

- Roast on top rack position in oven for 15 to 20 minutes until asparagus are browned but still crisp.

- Remove to platter and keep warm until ready to serve.
(Note: This dish can be made ahead and reheated in microwave.)

SERVES 8 TO 10

VINERY POTATOES

2 pounds potatoes or
1 (32-ounce) bag frozen,
shredded hash brown potatoes

2 tablespoons butter

1 pound fresh mushrooms,
finely chopped

1 small onion, grated

2 cups sour cream

2 (14.5-ounce) cans cream soup
(mushroom, onion, or celery)

Salt and freshly ground black
pepper to taste

- Preheat oven to 350°F.

- Peel and grate potatoes on large holes of box grater and keep covered with water until ready to use or thaw frozen hash browns.

- Sauté mushrooms and onions in butter until softened.

- If using fresh potatoes, drain and squeeze out water. In large mixing bowl, blend potatoes, onion, mushrooms, sour cream, soup, and salt and pepper.

- Place mixture in lightly buttered baking dish and bake 35 to 45 minutes until browned.

SERVES 8 TO 10

WARM CHOCOLATE CAKES

1 cup (2 sticks) plus 3 tablespoons unsalted butter

6 ounces good quality semisweet chocolate

3 whole eggs

3 egg yolks

⅓ cup sugar

1 teaspoon vanilla extract

⅓ cup all-purpose flour

¼ teaspoon salt

- Butter individual ramekins or muffin tin with 3 tablespoons butter.

- Over low heat, melt 1 cup butter and chocolate, stirring to blend. Cool slightly.

- In separate bowl, beat eggs, egg yolks, and sugar until thick and light yellow.

- Stir in cooled chocolate mixture.

- Add vanilla, flour, and salt, blending well. Mixture can stand covered at room temperature until ready to bake or will keep refrigerated up to one week.

- Fill ramekins or tin cups ⅔ full of batter, place on baking sheet, and bake in center of preheated 400°F oven for 12 minutes.

- Let cakes stand for 5 minutes; invert them onto individual dessert plates and serve immediately with any of the following: bourbon crème anglaise (recipe below), caramel sauce, vanilla ice cream, fresh berries, or whipped cream.

SERVES 8 TO 10

BOURBON CRÈME ANGLAISE

2 cups milk

5 egg yolks

⅔ cup sugar

⅛ teaspoon salt

1 teaspoon vanilla extract

¼ cup bourbon

- Scald milk in top of double boiler.

- In mixing bowl, beat together egg yolks, sugar, and salt.

- Slowly pour mixture into milk, whisking constantly.

- Continue cooking, stirring constantly until mixture thickens.

- Remove from heat and stir in vanilla and bourbon.

- Serve at room temperature with warm chocolate cakes. Can be refrigerated for 2 weeks and thinned with a little milk or cream if needed.

FALL

ADENA SPRINGS

FALL BRUNCH

Cream Cheese Pinwheels

Artichoke Soup

Chinese Chicken Salad

Pear Tart

The Adena Springs properties, initially in Woodford County and later with a division in Bourbon County, have continued the remarkable career path of owner Frank Stronach. A native of Austria, Stronach moved to Canada, where he washed dishes to support himself. He developed a tool and die business in a garage, which led to the creation of Magna International, a worldwide manufacturer of automobile parts.

As early as 1969, Stronach began buying high-end Thoroughbreds. He established a farm in Canada before branching into Kentucky in 1989. Adena Springs is named in tribute to the Adena Indians' historical connection to Central Kentucky.

Through 2006 Stronach/Adena Springs has been the leading Thoroughbred breeder in North America in racetrack earnings for four consecutive years. In the Thoroughbred industry's prestigious Eclipse Award voting, Stronach has won the breeder category four times and the owner category three times.

His connection to champions goes back more than a quarter-century, for he raced champion mare Glorious Song in partnership in 1980. More recently, Stronach's highlights at the racetrack include the Breeders' Cup Classic victories of Ghostzapper (2004) and Awesome Again (1998) and the 1997 Belmont Stakes victory of partnership-owned Touch Gold. Ghostzapper reigned as Horse of the Year in 2004. Similar to sportsmen of the past, Stronach has retired his best horses to stud at his own farms, and Awesome Again has joined the ranks of North America's leading stallions.

Stronach's Magna Entertainment has become one of the leading owners of racetracks, including the top-quality Santa Anita Park in California and Gulfstream Park in Florida.

CREAM CHEESE PINWHEELS

8 flour tortillas (8-inch size)

16 ounces cream cheese, softened

2 scallions minced

1 package Hidden Valley Ranch Salad Dressing mix

½ cup diced red pepper

½ cup diced celery

1 (3.5-ounce) can sliced black olives, drained

- Cut edges of tortillas to form squares.

- Mix cream cheese, scallions, and ranch dressing mix. Spread on tortillas.

- Sprinkle red pepper, celery, and olives evenly over prepared tortillas. Roll tortillas tightly, wrap each tortilla separately in plastic wrap, and refrigerate for at least 2 hours.

- Take plastic wrap off of rolls. Cut off ends of rolls and discard. Slice rolls into 1-inch discs and serve.

SERVES 8 TO 10

ARTICHOKE SOUP

1 stick (½ cup) butter

2 medium-sized white onions, thinly sliced

2 (28-ounce) cans diced tomatoes with juice

2 (14.5-ounce) cans chicken broth

2 (14-ounce) cans quartered artichoke hearts, packed in water

2 pints heavy cream

2 large bunches fresh basil, thinly sliced

Salt to taste

- Melt butter on low heat; add onions; sauté until transparent.

- Add diced tomatoes with juice, chicken broth, and drained artichoke hearts.

- Warm the cream and add basil and then add to tomato-artichoke mixture.

- Bring soup to a low boil; add salt to taste.

- Serve either hot or cold.

SERVES 8 TO 10

CHINESE CHICKEN SALAD

SALAD

6 cups chopped Napa cabbage

8 cups chopped Romaine lettuce

½ pound snow peas

½ cup carrots, julienned

½ cup zucchini, julienned

½ cup chopped scallions

½ cup chopped fresh cilantro

6 cups shredded chicken

½ cup sliced almonds, toasted

2 tablespoons sesame seeds, toasted

15 wontons, fried in 2 cups vegetable oil

DRESSING

¼ cup soy sauce

½ teaspoon fresh ground black pepper

¼ cup fresh lemon juice

1 tablespoon Asian sesame oil

2 tablespoons sugar

¼ cup olive oil

1 tablespoon distilled white vinegar

¼ teaspoon Tabasco sauce

1 teaspoon salt

- Combine cabbage, lettuce, snow peas, carrots, zucchini, scallions, and cilantro.

- Toss with shredded chicken, toasted almonds, and sesame seeds.

- Combine all ingredients of dressing recipe, and mix into salad.

- Top with fried wontons.

SERVES 8 TO 10

PEAR TART

2 cups all-purpose (plain) flour

¼ teaspoon salt

2 tablespoons vegetable shortening

1 stick (½ cup) unsalted butter

4 tablespoons cold water

- Preheat oven to 425°F.

- In food processor, pulse to blend flour, salt, shortening, butter and cold water until dough starts to form round ball.

- Remove dough from processor and roll into ball, cover with plastic wrap, and refrigerate for at least 1 hour.

- Once chilled, roll out dough and fit in 9-inch tart pan with removable bottom.

- Line tart shell with aluminum foil and place dried beans on top. This helps keep tart shell from bubbling up.

- Bake 10 to 12 minutes, remove, and cool.

POACHED PEARS

6 firm, ripe pears

½ cup sugar

1 cup water

- To poach pears, bring water and sugar to a boil.

- Peel pears, stand them up in syrup mixture, and simmer for 5 minutes. Remove from water and cool.

- To make cream filling, cream the butter and sugar with electric mixer; add egg, almonds, rum, flour, and vanilla extract; beat until smooth.

CREAM FILLING

1 stick (½ cup) softened unsalted butter

½ cup sugar

1 egg

1 cup slivered almonds

4 tablespoons dark rum

1 tablespoon flour

1 teaspoon vanilla extract

1 cup apricot preserves

- Spread filling evenly over baked tart shell.

- Slice pears in decorative manner, and place over cream filling.

- Warm up 1 cup of apricot preserves; brush preserves over pears, reserving some to brush on surface after baking.

- Preheat oven to 375°F and bake for 35 to 40 minutes or until cream filling is set.

SERVES 8 TO 10

CASTLETON LYONS

FALL LUNCHEON

Smoked Irish Salmon and Crab Parcels

Arugula Salad with Classic French Vinaigrette

Castleton Lyons Boneless Leg of Lamb with Mint Sauce

Parsnip Purée

Steamed Brussels Sprouts with Orange Butter

Tarte Lascombes with Crème Fraiche

Champion horses of three breeds have created a proud history for the property now known as Castleton Lyons near Lexington. U.S. Senator, Attorney General, and Vice President John Breckinridge founded the farm in 1793. By 1812 it was named Castleton by David Castleman, who settled there with his bride, Mary Breckinridge. Nearly a century later Wall Street tycoon James R. Keene owned the farm. He bred eleven Thoroughbred champions at Castleton, including the great, unbeaten Colin. Succeeding owners included Frances and Frederick Van Lennep. Under their watch, Saddlebred immortal Wing Commander was bred there, as well as numerous top Standardbreds, such as Speedy Scot and Race Time.

In 2001 Dr. Tony Ryan, founder of the European airline Ryanair, purchased Castleton. Ryan appended the name Lyons in recognition of the farm's new affiliation with his estate back in his native Ireland, Lyons Demesne. Ryan extensively renovated the original 1840s Greek Revival mansion at his Kentucky farm and imported a massive wrought-iron gate from London for the entrance to the main house. However, the farm's immaculate stone fences and spacious paddocks along Iron Works Pike, long one of the most scenic drives in the Bluegrass, remain in their historic handsomeness.

Unabashedly harboring the ambition of "emulating and eclipsing the success of the farm's glorious Thoroughbred past," Ryan made Castleton Lyons home to Thoroughbreds for the first time in some ninety years. He quickly launched an innovative breeding and marketing program and gathered a band of young stallions. Early in the twenty-first century this line-up included Malibu Moon, sire of champion Declan's Moon, and the phenomenal Bernstein, already the sire of seven group 1 winners, both of whom are helping Ryan realize his goal.

SMOKED IRISH SALMON AND CRAB PARCELS

½ pound sliced smoked salmon

½ pound lump crab meat

½ cup mayonnaise

Juice from ½ of a lemon

Salt and pepper to taste

Fresh parsley and lemon slices
for garnish

- Grease 6 to 8 4-ounce ramekins with oil or cooking spray and line with plastic wrap, leaving plenty of excess wrap.

- Line each ramekin with slices of smoked salmon.

- Combine crab meat, mayonnaise, lemon juice, salt, and pepper. Divide crab mixture evenly among ramekins, folding excess salmon over the top. Bring sides of plastic wrap over and press down firmly.

- Refrigerate 1 to 2 hours or more.

- Open plastic wrap, invert onto salad plate, and peel off wrap. Garnish with parsley and lemon slice. Serve immediately.

SERVES 6 TO 8

ARUGULA SALAD WITH CLASSIC FRENCH VINAIGRETTE

SALAD

2 (5-ounce) packages of
Arugula greens

FRENCH VINAIGRETTE

¼ cup red wine vinegar

¾ cup extra virgin olive oil

1 tablespoon Dijon mustard

Salt and pepper to taste

Juice of one lemon

Pinch of herbes de Provence

- Whisk together all dressing ingredients until combined and thickened. Toss with greens and serve immediately.

SERVES 6 TO 8

CASTLETON LYONS BONELESS LEG OF LAMB (WITH MINT JELLY)

3–4 large cloves of garlic,
peeled and crushed

2 tablespoons soy sauce

¼ cup Dijon mustard

Small handful of fragrant herbs
such as mint, rosemary, thyme,
and oregano

1 tablespoon cracked black pepper

2 tablespoons freshly squeezed
lemon juice

½ cup (1 stick) unsalted butter,
melted

1 boneless leg of lamb, large
enough to serve 8 to 10

- Preheat oven to 450°F.

- Combine all seasoning ingredients except butter and blend for 1 minute in a food processor. While continuing to blend, gradually add melted butter through food processor chute until mixture is the consistency of mayonnaise.

- Coat leg of lamb liberally with mixture and refrigerate at least two hours or overnight.

- Roast leg of lamb fat side up 15 minutes per pound for medium rare or until meat thermometer inserted at thickest point reaches 130°F.

- Remove from oven and let rest for 10 to 15 minutes before carving.

- Serve mint jelly on the side.

SERVES 8 TO 10

PARSNIP PURÉE

2 pounds parsnips, peeled
and cubed

1 cup heavy cream

½ stick unsalted butter

Salt and freshly ground white
pepper to taste

- Boil parsnips, covered, 30 to 40 minutes until very soft. Drain.

- Carefully heat cream and butter in small saucepan or in microwave in glass measuring cup.

- Whip parsnips with electric mixer, gradually adding cream and butter mixture to desired consistency. (Note: You may not use all of the cream mixture. For creamiest results use a food processor.)

- Season with salt and pepper. If not serving immediately, cover with plastic wrap that touches surface of puree so a crust does not form.

SERVES 6 TO 8

BRUSSELS SPROUTS WITH ORANGE BUTTER

2 pounds fresh Brussels sprouts

½ cup (1 stick) unsalted butter

Juice and zest of 1 orange

1 teaspoon Dijon mustard

Cracked black pepper to taste

- Remove outer leaves and trim bases of Brussels sprouts.

- Rinse and score stems with an "X" to cook more evenly.

- Steam for 5 to 10 minutes until just tender and still bright green.

- Melt butter in large sauté pan; add orange juice, zest, and Dijon mustard.

- Add Brussels sprouts to the sauce and coat.

- Outer leaves of the sprouts will begin to caramelize, yielding a lovely brown color.

- Serve immediately.

SERVES 6 TO 8

TARTE LASCOMBES WITH CRÈME FRAICHE

4–6 large tart cooking apples
(Granny Smith, Braeburn,
or Gala)

½ cup (1 stick) unsalted butter

½ cup sugar

1 cup Chateau Lascombes wine
(or another sweet red wine)

10–12-inch round of pastry

- Preheat oven to 350°F.

- Peel, core, and cut apples into large chunks.

- In a large saucepan on medium heat, melt the butter, swirl in the sugar, and add apples.

- When the apple juices turn dark brown, add the wine and cook until liquid is reduced by half. Pour into deep-dish pie pan.

- Cover the pan with pastry, crimp edges, and make slits in top. Place in a 350°F oven and bake about 20 minutes or until crust is golden brown.

- Remove from oven and immediately invert onto platter for serving. Cut with pizza cutter and serve with warm crème fraiche or whipped cream.

SERVES 6 TO 8

CRESTFIELD FARM

THANKSGIVING DINNER

Brandied Cranberries

Winter Sprouts with Chestnuts

Yeast Rolls

Southern Cornbread Dressing

Sweet Potato Supreme Soufflé

Baked Parmesan-Herb Oysters

Make-Ahead Mashed Potatoes

Brined Thanksgiving Turkey

Chocolate Pecan Pie with a Shot

Mr. and Mrs. Robert Estill Courtney established Crestfield Farm in 1956 when they purchased 130 acres on Royster Road in Lexington. Thirty years later they needed to expand and purchased Stonebridge Farm on nearby Cleveland Road. By that time, Crestfield's distinctions included the breeding of New York Handicap Triple winner Fit to Fight, who was purchased as a yearling by Paul Mellon and raced in his colors. The colt's dam, partnership-owned Hasty Queen II, was named Broodmare of the Year.

Crestfield is a family-run operation that includes the Courtneys' sons, Robert Jr. and Tom. In addition to maintaining its own broodmare band and sale yearlings, the farm boards mares, raises foals, and preps yearlings for clients. Crestfield has sold five horses that went on to be champions in the United States, England, and Ireland. These include Action This Day, who was raised for longtime client Jaime S. Carrion. Action This Day won the Breeders' Cup Juvenile in 2003 and was named the year's champion two-year-old colt.

Robert Courtney Sr. is a past president of the Kentucky Thoroughbred Farm Managers' Club, which named him Farm Manager of the Year in 1970. He also is a past president of the Thoroughbred Club of America and was named that organization's guest of honor at its annual Testimonial Dinner in 2003.

BRANDIED CRANBERRIES

4 cups of fresh or frozen
(thawed) cranberries

2 cups sugar

4 tablespoons brandy or cognac

- Place berries in single layer in shallow baking dish, sprinkle with sugar, and cover dish tightly with heavy-duty aluminum foil.

- Bake in preheated oven at 350°F for 1 hour.

- Cool berries; then mix in about 4 tablespoons of brandy (or more to taste), and sprinkle lightly with additional sugar. Refrigerate until ready to serve.

SERVES 10 TO 12 (2 CUPS)

WINTER SPROUTS WITH CHESTNUTS

2 pounds Brussel sprouts

3 tablespoons unsalted butter

1 teaspoon coarse salt

1 teaspoon black pepper

2 cups water

1½ cups heavy cream

1 cup bottled roasted chestnuts,
coarsely crumbled

- Wash Brussels sprouts; trim ends off. Using a sharp knife, make a small "X" in the base of each sprout.

- Bring butter, salt, pepper, and 2 cups water to boil over high heat in deep, heavy skillet. Add sprouts, cover, and simmer until tender (6 to 8 minutes).

- Remove lid and boil over moderately high heat until water is evaporated and sprouts are slightly brown.

- Add cream a little at a time and bring back to boil.

- Add chestnuts and reduce heat to simmer until all are heated, about 2 minutes. Serve immediately.

SERVES 10 TO 12

YEAST ROLLS

½ cup boiling water

½ cup vegetable shortening

½ cup sugar

¾ teaspoon salt

1 egg

1 package dry yeast

½ cup lukewarm water

3 cups bread flour

6 tablespoons unsalted butter,
melted

- In large bowl, pour boiling water over shortening, sugar, and salt. Stir until blended and cool. Beat egg slightly and add to shortening mixture.

- Sprinkle yeast over lukewarm water in glass measuring cup, allow to dissolve, and stir gently. Stir yeast into mixture.

- Add flour, mixing in a little at a time, and blend well. Cover bowl with plastic wrap and refrigerate 6 hours or overnight.

- Knead dough gently on floured surface about 2 minutes. Roll out about ½-inch thick and cut with a 2-inch biscuit cutter. Dip rolls in melted butter, fold in half, and place in buttered 10x14-inch pan. Allow rolls to rise 1 to 1½ hours, until almost double in size.

- Bake at 400°F for 12 minutes or until golden brown.

MAKES 30 TO 36 ROLLS

SWEET POTATO SUPREME SOUFFLÉ

4 cups sweet potatoes
    (about 5 sweet potatoes)

2 egg yolks

½ cup unsalted butter, melted

1 cup sugar

1½ teaspoons vanilla extract

2 egg whites

TOPPING:

1 cup brown sugar

½ cup all-purpose flour

1 cup chopped pecans

½ cup unsalted butter, softened

- Peel sweet potatoes, cut in large chunks, and boil in salted water until just fork tender. Remove from water and mash until all lumps are smooth.

- Beat egg yolks and add to potatoes.

- Melt butter and add sugar and vanilla. Stir into potatoes.

- Beat egg whites until soft peaks form and fold into potato mixture.

- Place potatoes in buttered 3-quart rectangular baking dish and cover with topping.

- To prepare the topping, in small bowl, mix brown sugar, flour, and pecans. Add butter and mix. Spread by spoonfuls on potatoes. (Topping may be assembled 2 days ahead, covered, and refrigerated.)

- Bake potatoes at 350°F for 30 to 45 minutes until topping is melted and potatoes are hot.

SERVES 10 TO 12

SOUTHERN CORNBREAD DRESSING

¼ cup butter

2 cups celery, finely chopped

1½ teaspoons sage (optional)

1½ cups onion, finely chopped

¾ cup bell pepper, finely chopped

½ cup flat-leaf parsley

2½ teaspoons salt

½ teaspoon black pepper

1½ teaspoons celery seed

5 cups golden cornbread

6 slices whole wheat bread, crumbled

4 eggs, slightly beaten

2 cups chicken broth

- Melt butter in pan and sauté celery, onion, and bell pepper until tender.

- Add parsley and seasonings.

- Cut crusts off of cornbread and crumble. Repeat with wheat bread. Mix with sautéed vegetables.

- Add eggs and chicken broth; mix well. Add more broth if consistency seems dry.

- Place mixture in 2-quart rectangular Pyrex casserole dish or mold into individual dressing balls and place on baking sheet.

- Bake at 350°F for 45 minutes.

SERVES 12

GOLDEN CORNBREAD

2 cups yellow cornmeal

1½ cups all-purpose flour

3 tablespoons and 1 teaspoon baking powder

1½ teaspoons salt

2 eggs, slightly beaten

2 cups milk

4 tablespoons melted shortening

- Sift together dry ingredients in bowl and add egg, milk, and shortening. Mix thoroughly and pour into greased 9x12-inch pan. Bake at 425°F for 25 minutes or until golden brown.

BAKED PARMESAN-HERB OYSTERS

½ cup butter

3 slices bacon, fried and crumbled, reserving 1 tablespoon of drippings

1 tablespoon of drippings

1 large onion, finely chopped

3 cloves garlic, minced

2 tablespoons chopped fresh flat-leaf parsley

½ teaspoon thyme

¾ teaspoon oregano

⅛ teaspoon cayenne pepper

Salt and pepper to taste

4 dozen oysters, strained (reserve liquid)

1 cup bread crumbs from lightly toasted bread slices

Grated fresh Parmesan cheese

- Melt butter and bacon drippings in pan and sauté onion until translucent.

- Add garlic, herbs, seasonings, and blend.

- Add oysters and gently sauté until oysters curl at the edges.

- Add bread crumbs and bacon, mixing gently.

- Divide oyster mixture into individual ramekins or use a 9x13-inch baking dish, sprinkle top with Parmesan cheese, and bake at 350°F for 10 minutes for the ramekins and 15 minutes for the large dish.

SERVES 10 TO 12

MAKE-AHEAD MASHED POTATOES

10–12 potatoes, peeled and cooked

8 ounces cream cheese, room temperature

1 cup sour cream, room temperature

4 teaspoons salt

½ stick unsalted butter

1 beaten egg

- Mash potatoes with potato masher.

- Combine potatoes with cream cheese, sour cream, salt, butter, and egg and mix in electric mixer.

- Spoon into greased 9x13-inch casserole dish. (Potatoes may be refrigerated up to two days at this point.)

- Before baking, bring potatoes to room temperature, dot with butter, and bake at 350°F for 30 minutes.

SERVES 10 TO 12

CHOCOLATE PECAN PIE WITH A SHOT

1 flakey pie crust

FILLING

3 tablespoons all-purpose flour

½ cup unsalted butter, melted

½ cup sugar

½ cup dark corn syrup

2 large eggs

2 tablespoons Kentucky bourbon

¼ teaspoon salt

2 cups pecans, toasted & chopped

1 cup semisweet chocolate, chopped

1 egg with 1 teaspoon water

- Preheat oven to 350°F.

- On a lightly floured surface, roll out pie crust, fit into a 9-inch pie pan, crimp the edges, and place in freezer for 15 minutes.

- Line pie crust with parchment paper, and fill with pie weights or dried beans. Bake for 20 minutes; then remove the paper and pie weights and allow crust to cool.

- By hand, combine flour, butter, sugar, corn syrup, eggs, bourbon, and salt in medium bowl. Stir in chopped pecans and chocolate. Pour into pie crust.

- Whisk egg and water and brush over the edges of the pie.

- Bake for 40 minutes. Allow to cool. Serve with a dollop of whipped cream.

SERVES 6 TO 8

BRINED THANKSGIVING TURKEY

FOR BRINING

8 quarts water

2 cups of kosher salt

1 18-pound turkey, thawed

- To ensure a moist turkey, it is best to brine the bird before roasting.

- Stir together 8 quarts water and 2 cups kosher salt in a clean 5-gallon bucket or container with a cover. If desired, you can add a bit of sugar and/or spices to the brine.

- Add the raw turkey, cover, and chill in refrigerator for a minimum of 10 hours. If you soak the bird for 24 hours, reduce the amount of salt to 1 cup.

- Remove turkey and air dry in refrigerator for approximately 2 hours.

TO ROAST

1 turkey, brined

1 stick unsalted butter

Salt, pepper, and poultry seasoning, to taste

1 lemon

- Preheat oven to 450°F.

- Spray roasting pan with cooking spray and place ½ cup water in bottom. "Paint" the bird with a stick of melted butter, salt and pepper; then tie legs with string. Place meat thermometer along the breast meat, being careful not to touch the bone.

- Slice lemon in half and insert both halves in cavity along with salt, pepper, and poultry seasoning.

- Form an aluminum foil tent to cover breast of turkey. (You will place this over turkey when you turn down heat to 325°F.)

- Add water to cover the bottom of roasting pan. Place turkey uncovered in the oven at 450°F for 30 minutes.

- Turn down heat to 325°F and continue to bake. Remove turkey when thermometer registers 162°F. Cook a 14- to 16-pound turkey approximately 2½ hours, a 22-pound turkey 3½ hours.

- Allow turkey to rest for 30 minutes before carving.

SERVES 12

DARBY DAN FARM

AFTER A DOVE SHOOT

Mixed Greens with Fruit and Blue Cheese

Grilled Doves

Roasted Beef Ribs

Darby Dan Potatoes

Country Green Beans

Texas Sheet Cake

More than a century ago Colonel E.R. Bradley established Idle Hour Stock Farm on property now known as Darby Dan Farm. Bradley rose to racing fame as owner of four Kentucky Derby winners while establishing a broodmare band whose influence continues many generations later.

Some years after Bradley's death, John W. Galbreath, a singular sportsman and entrepreneur from Columbus, Ohio, purchased a section of the farm just west of Lexington in 1957. Galbreath renamed the property Darby Dan and built upon the record of success. He gathered some of the world's best racehorses, such as Ribot, Sea-Bird, and Swaps, to stand as Darby Dan stallions, and he bred winners of all three of America's Triple Crown races, including Kentucky Derby winners Chateaugay and Proud Clarion.

When Roberto carried Galbreath's colors to victory in the 1972 Epsom Derby, the Darby Dan influence was extended internationally. Returned to the farm, Roberto launched a renowned succession of top male racehorses and stallions that included Brian's Time, Silver Hawk, Kris S., and Dynaformer, sire of the ill-fated Kentucky Derby winner Barbaro. Other major winners bred and raced by Galbreath included Graustark and Primonetta, plus Breeders' Cup Classic winner Proud Truth.

Following the deaths of John W. Galbreath and his son Dan, a grandson, John W. Phillips, moved from Columbus to Lexington to continue the farm. Proving the glory days were not relegated to the past, Phillips and his mother, Mrs. Jody Phillips, bred and raced the champion turf mare and Breeders' Cup winner Soaring Softly. Responding to changes in the industry, Darby Dan has been converted from an operation that breeds primarily to race to an integrated source of client services in racing and selling while maintaining a distinguished stallion roster.

MIXED GREENS WITH FRUIT AND BLUE CHEESE

2 (6-ounce) bags baby spinach

2 (6-ounce) bags romaine lettuce

3 gala apples, chopped with skins attached

½ cup blueberrries

½ cup toasted pine nuts

6–8 ounces blue cheese crumbles

DRESSING:

½ cup olive oil

¼ cup red wine vinegar

2 tablespoons of sugar

- Combine oil, vinegar, and sugar; shake well.
- Toss all salad ingredients with oil and vinegar dressing and serve.

SERVES 8 TO 10

GRILLED DOVES

8 dressed doves

MARINADE

½ cup soy sauce

½ cup vegetable oil

½ cup white vinegar

½ cup lemon juice

- Whisk together marinade ingredients and pour into glass dish. Place 8 dressed doves in the marinade for at least 2 hours to no more than 8 hours. Cover. (Note: This recipe also works for doves that have been frozen then thawed.)
- Preheat grill to medium heat.
- Grill over medium heat for 20 to 25 minutes, turning as needed to prevent burning. Serve immediately.

SERVES 6 TO 8

ROASTED BEEF RIBS

6 beef ribs (5–6 pounds)

MARINADE

1 cup vegetable oil

½ cup Worcestershire sauce

Juice of 2 lemons

1 teaspoon salt

1 teaspoon garlic salt

1 teaspoon black pepper

2 medium onions, sliced

- Trim fat from ribs. Place in 9x13-inch baking dish.
- Combine remaining ingredients. Pour marinade over ribs. Cover and refrigerate overnight.
- Preheat oven to 350°F.
- Drain marinade and discard.
- In oven, bake ribs at 350°F for 30 minutes or until tender. While ribs are in the oven, start a charcoal fire on the grill. Remove ribs from oven and place on grills over hot coals.
- Grill ribs 10 minutes on each side, or until crisp and brown.

SERVES 6 TO 8

DARBY DAN POTATOES

6 Yukon gold, California new (white), or red potatoes

1 tablespoon olive oil

½ teaspoon crushed rosemary or thyme

Salt and pepper to taste

1 small clove garlic, minced

- Blanch potatoes for 10 minutes. Slice lengthwise in ¼- or ⅙-inch pieces.
- Spray cooking spray into ovenproof pan or use nonstick pan.
- Layer sliced potatoes in pan.
- Drizzle olive oil over potatoes. Add crushed rosemary or thyme and salt and pepper. Sprinkle garlic.
- Bake at 375°F for 1 hour.

SERVES 6 TO 8

COUNTRY GREEN BEANS

2–3 pounds fresh green beans

3–4 slices bacon (uncooked)

1 tablespoon (heaping) bacon drippings

1 large onion, chopped

1 tablespoon (heaping) sugar

¼ teaspoon red pepper flakes

Salt and pepper to taste

- Pop ends off beans and cut into bite-sized pieces. Rinse in cold water.
- Place in large pan with just enough water to cover.
- Cut bacon into pieces and add to beans with rest of ingredients.
- Bring beans to boil. Reduce heat and simmer (covered) for 1½ hours, adding water if necessary.

SERVES 6 TO 8

TEXAS SHEET CAKE

2 cups all-purpose flour

2 cups sugar

¼ teaspoon salt

1 teaspoon baking soda

1 cup (2 sticks) unsalted butter

1 cup water

3 tablespoons (heaping) cocoa

½ cup sour cream

2 eggs

1 teaspoon vanilla

ICING

½ cup (1 stick) unsalted butter

6 tablespoons milk

3 tablespoons (heaping) cocoa

1 (1-pound) box powdered sugar

1 teaspoon vanilla

1 cup chopped pecans

- Preheat oven to 350°F.
- Sift flour, sugar, salt, and baking soda together.
- In saucepan, melt butter over medium heat. Add water and cocoa and bring to a low boil.
- Remove from heat; allow to cool slightly. Beat in sour cream, eggs, and vanilla.
- Add dry ingredients. Beat until well blended. Pour into greased 9x13-inch rectangular baking dish.
- Bake at 350°F for 20 minutes.
- Frost with icing while cake is warm.

- Combine butter, milk, and cocoa. Bring to boil and cook 2 minutes, slowly stirring.
- Remove from heat and beat in powdered sugar and vanilla.
- Stir in chopped nuts and pour over warm cake.

SERVES 8 TO 10

HURRICANE HALL

FALL BRUNCH

Spinach and Strawberry Salad

Shrimp and Grits, Fayette Style

Smothered Quail or Doves

Sweet Potato and Black Pepper Biscuits

Broiled Tomatoes

Pumpkin Cream Cheese Pie

Distinguished since the eighteenth century, Hurricane Hall entered a new, modern, and vigorous chapter in 2005 thanks to a group of experienced horsemen. Ben P. Walden Jr., president of Hurricane Hall, grew up in the Kentucky horse business and has operated Vinery and Gracefield farms. His partners are Patrick Madden Jr., from the family long associated with Hamburg Place; Brad Kelley, also owner of Bluegrass Farm and a former board member at Churchill Downs; and David Hanley, a successful trainer in his native Ireland as well as in North America.

The partners established a stallion operation, beginning at a high level. They started with stallions Artie Schiller, winner of the 2005 Breeders' Cup Mile, and Bellamy Road, winner of the 2005 Wood Memorial and that year's Kentucky Derby favorite. The farm, located on Georgetown Road in northern Fayette County, is a full-service facility and includes a one-mile Polytrack training oval as well as grass training gallops.

Respectful of the property's history, Walden and partners have renovated the six-bedroom home, for which the farm is named, into a guesthouse. Few farms offer a guesthouse with such distinction. In the volume *Antebellum Houses of the Bluegrass*, architectural historian Clay Lancaster describes Hurricane Hall as "the most engaging residence in Fayette County of which a part predates 1800." The core of the house dates from 1794, and Samuel Loughead built the original, a Federal brick house reminiscent of Virginia styles. In 1801 the house was purchased by Roger Quarles, who added a Kentucky Federal wing. Quarles' grandson added yet another feature, a Greek Revival wing, in 1840. Additions made by its succession of owners give Hurricane Hall a unique blend of styles.

SHRIMP AND GRITS, FAYETTE STYLE

2 cups milk

2 cups chicken broth

1 cup quick grits

½ cup white cheddar cheese, grated

1 cup Parmesan cheese, grated

Salt and pepper to taste

1 beaten egg

½ pound bacon

2 teaspoons olive oil or bacon grease

2 packages (5 ounces each) sliced almonds

2 red bell peppers, seeded and diced

1 yellow bell pepper, seeded and diced

3 garlic cloves, minced

2 teaspoons hot sauce

2 pounds medium shrimp

1 cup sharp cheddar cheese, shredded

3 bunches scallions, chopped

- Bring milk and broth to boil. Add grits, reduce heat, cover, stirring periodically for 5 to 7 minutes.

- Remove from heat and add white cheddar cheese, ½ cup Parmesan cheese, salt, pepper, and egg. Pour into 9x13-inch greased casserole.

- Cook bacon and crumble.

- Sauté almonds, diced peppers, and garlic in olive oil or bacon grease until vegetables are slightly softened. Add hot sauce and shrimp; cook for an additional 3 to 5 minutes or until shrimp are pink.

- Add this mixture to grits and top with bacon, sharp cheddar cheese, other ½ cup Parmesan, and chopped green onions.

- Bake at 325°F until hot, or about 20 minutes. Can be made ahead and frozen.

SERVES 6 TO 8

SPINACH AND STRAWBERRY SALAD

1 large bunch of spinach
(enough for 8)

1 (16-ounce) container
of strawberries, sliced

2 small red onions, sliced thin

1¼ cups sugar

¼ to ½ cup of almonds

1 teaspoon dry mustard

1 teaspoon salt

⅓ cup red wine vinegar

1 cup vegetable oil

1 tablespoon poppy seeds

- Mix spinach, strawberries, and 1 small thin-sliced red onion.

- Melt ½ cup sugar in a skillet, pour in almonds. Stir constantly until the sugar and almonds begin to brown slightly.

- Put the nuts on a piece of waxed paper. After cooling, break almonds into bite-sized pieces. (Sugared almonds keep 1 month in an airtight container.)

- In blender or food processor, blend ¾ cup sugar, dry mustard, salt, red wine vinegar, and 1 small sliced red onion.

- While the blender or food processor is on, slowly pour in vegetable oil and poppy seeds. (Dressing can be refrigerated for 1 month).

- Toss dressing on salad and top with sugared almonds.

SERVES 8

SWEET POTATO AND BLACK PEPPER BISCUITS

2 cups unsifted all-purpose flour

¼ teaspoon salt

2 teaspoons baking powder

½ teaspoon baking soda

1 teaspoon sugar

½ teaspoon cracked black pepper

¾ cup (1½ sticks) unsalted butter

1 cup cooked sweet potatoes,
puréed

2 tablespoons heavy cream

- Preheat oven to 425°F.

- In large bowl, combine all dry ingredients.

- Using pastry blender, food processor, or your fingertips, cut butter into flour mixture until mixture resembles coarse crumbles.

- Stir in sweet potato purée and cream and mix gently until soft dough forms. You may need to add extra cream. Do not overmix.

- Turn out dough onto lightly floured surface. Knead gently 5 times.

- Pat out dough to ½-inch thickness.

- Using a 2-inch biscuit cutter, cut dough and place on ungreased baking sheet.

- Bake at 425°F until lightly browned, approximately 12 to 15 minutes.

MAKES APPROXIMATELY 24 BISCUITS

BROILED TOMATOES

6 fresh tomatoes, unpeeled

6 tablespoons sherry

¾ teaspoon dill weed

1 teaspoon black pepper

6 tablespoons mayonnaise

8 tablespoons Parmesan cheese, grated

- Remove core from each tomato. Cut in half.

- Place cut side up on cookie sheet. Pierce each tomato several times with a fork.

- Sprinkle each half with sherry, dill weed, and pepper.

- Broil for 2 to 3 minutes.

- Top each half with a mixture of mayonnaise and Parmesan cheese and return to broiler for 1 minute.

- Serve immediately.

SERVES 12

SMOTHERED QUAIL OR DOVES

4 quail or 8 dove breasts

Salt and pepper to taste

3–4 tablespoons unsalted butter

½ cup water

¼ cup dry sherry
    or ½ cup white wine

3 tablespoons lemon juice

Tabasco sauce to taste

2 teaspoons Worcestershire sauce

1 tablespoon all-purpose flour

½–1 cup heavy cream

½ pound sliced mushrooms, sautéed

12 ounces wild rice, cooked

- Season birds with salt and pepper and brown lightly in butter.

- Add water, wine, lemon juice, and other seasonings. Cover and cook over low heat until birds are tender (1 to 1½ hours). Remove.

- Blend flour into cream and stir into sauce in pan. Cook until sauce slightly thickens. Add sautéed mushrooms. Serve with wild rice.

- Dish may be cooked ahead, refrigerated, and reheated in a chafing dish or slow oven.

SERVES 4

PUMPKIN CREAM CHEESE PIE

1½ cups fine crumbs from
graham crackers

1 cup fine crumbs from
ginger snaps

4 tablespoons unsalted butter

1 (8-ounce) package cream cheese
(at room temperature)

¾ cup brown sugar

2 tablespoons all-purpose flour

2 teaspoons cinnamon

1 teaspoon ginger

½ teaspoon salt

¼ teaspoon nutmeg

1 (16-ounce) can pumpkin

1 (5.33-ounce) can evaporated milk

3 eggs

TOPPING

2 tablespoons unsalted butter

¾ cup almonds

⅓ cup brown sugar

- Preheat oven to 375°F.

- Combine graham crackers, ginger snaps, and melted butter. Press mixture into pie pan. (Makes two pie shells.)

- Bake for 3 to 5 minutes. Cool completely.

- Mix cream cheese, brown sugar, flour, cinnamon, ginger, salt, and nutmeg together.

- Add pumpkin, evaporated milk, and eggs. Mix and pour into pie shells.

- Bake 30 minutes at 375°F.

- For topping, combine butter, almonds, and brown sugar.

- Put topping on pies and continue to bake 5 more minutes.

MAKES 2 PIES

MT. BRILLIANT FARM

FALL DINNER

Garlic-Chile Soup with Tortilla Strips

Sautéed Quail and Fried Onion Rings over Mesclun

Ancho-Honey-Glazed Beef Tenderloin with Cilantro-Lime Butter

Jalapeño Cheese Grits and Sautéed Sugar Snap Peas

Cowboy Chocolate Cake with Warm Chocolate Sauce

Greg and Becky Goodman's Mt. Brilliant Farm embraces a unique series of historic structures and natural wonders. The last barn to house Man o' War is on part of the property acquired from the Jeffords family. Goodman has had the barn renovated, and its stall doors bear brass names from the glorious past, including those of Man o' War and his greatest son, War Admiral. Elsewhere on the farm stands a monument to another champion racehorse, the storied Domino.

A unique natural element on Mt. Brilliant is Russell Cave, site of an underground spring. While Russell Cave today gives its name to a well-known thoroughfare winding through the countryside north of Lexington, in the nineteenth century the name was associated with a famous duel that took place there in 1843 between Cassius Marcellus Clay and Samuel Brown.

Mt. Brilliant's history also was touched by none other than Thomas Jefferson. It was Jefferson who granted acreage to the original owner, William Russell, in recognition of his brother's military service during the French and Indian War. In later years Mt. Brilliant was owned by James Ben Ali Haggin, a Kentucky horse breeder who also owned vast ranching and mining properties in California and South America.

The Goodmans have developed new chapters to the distinguished farm's association with the Thoroughbred. Early on, success was underscored when Dreaming of Anna, daughter of the farm-owned mare Justenuffheart, won the Breeders' Cup Juvenile Fillies and the Eclipse Award for her division.

Another tradition of Mt. Brilliant over generations has been its floral beauty, and the Goodmans have designed a formal English flower garden as well as a vineyard and a kitchen garden of berries, vegetables, and herbs.

GARLIC-CHILE SOUP

3 heads of garlic

1–2 chipotle chiles
in adobo sauce

1 small onion, diced

1 tablespoon olive oil

1 teaspoon cumin

8 cups chicken broth

6 sprigs cilantro

Salt and pepper to taste

Juice of 1 lime

Corn tortilla strips (recipe below)

- Preheat oven to 400°F.

- Slice garlic heads in half; drizzle with olive oil. Wrap in foil and roast 30 to 45 minutes. When cool, squeeze garlic cloves from their skins.

- Remove seeds from chipotle chiles.

- Sauté onions in pot until soft, sprinkle with cumin, and cook until fragrant.

- Put onion mixture in blender with garlic and chipotles, and purée.

- Transfer purée to onion pot and over medium-low heat cook 1 to 2 minutes.

- Add chicken broth along with 6 cilantro sprigs. Bring to boil; then let simmer 20 to 30 minutes.

- Remove cilantro sprigs. Season to taste with salt and pepper. Add lime juice to soup and garnish with baked corn tortilla strips.

SERVES 6

TORTILLA STRIPS

4 corn tortillas

¼ cup vegetable oil

Salt

- Preheat oven to 375°F.

- Slice tortillas into ¼-inch strips.

- Toss lightly with vegetable oil and sprinkle with salt.

- Spread on a sheet pan and bake until golden and crisp, approximately 5 to 10 minutes.

SERVES 6

SAUTÉED QUAIL

6 (5-ounce) split breasted quail

Salt and pepper

2 tablespoons clarified butter

2 tablespoons vegetable oil

8–10 ounces mesclun

- Rinse quail in cold water and dry thoroughly. Season with salt and pepper.

- Over medium high heat, sauté quail in butter and oil, skin side first, 4 to 5 minutes.

- Place quail over individual beds of mesclun; then top with one or two fried onion rings. Sprinkle orange cumin vinaigrette over top and serve.

SERVES 6

FRIED ONION RINGS

1 Vidalia onion

1 cup buttermilk

1 cup flour

½ teaspoon garlic powder

½ teaspoon paprika

¼ teaspoon cayenne pepper

1 teaspoon black pepper

1 teaspoon salt

3 cups peanut oil

- Thinly slice Vidalia onion and let soak in buttermilk for 1 hour.

- Heat oil to 375°F in a saucepan.

- Mix flour with the next five ingredients.

- Remove onion rings from buttermilk and dredge in flour mixture. Drop a few at a time into hot oil and fry until golden.

SERVES 6

ORANGE CUMIN VINAIGRETTE

2 tablespoons shallots, minced

1 tablespoon fresh lime juice

1 teaspoon Dijon mustard

½ cup fresh orange juice

½ teaspoon garlic, minced

2 tablespoons honey

2 tablespoons ground cumin

3 tablespoons red wine vinegar

¼ teaspoon cayenne pepper

¾ cup olive oil

- Place first 9 ingredients in food processor and pulse. With motor still running, slowly add olive oil until mixture is emulsified.

SERVES 6

ANCHO-HONEY-GLAZED BEEF TENDERLOIN
WITH CILANTRO-LIME BUTTER

1 beef tenderloin (6–7 pounds)

Salt and pepper

Vegetable oil

Cilantro-lime butter

- Allow tenderloin to rest out of refrigerator for 1 hour before cooking.

- Preheat oven to 450°F. Place beef in a shallow roasting pan or broiler pan and season with salt and pepper to taste and brush with vegetable oil.

- For medium rare, cook beef until internal temperature (use meat thermometer) is 120°F. Near the end of cooking, brush on Ancho-Honey glaze.

- When beef is done, remove from oven and allow to rest 10 minutes.

- Pour cilantro-lime butter over tenderloin; slice and serve.

SERVES 6

ANCHO-HONEY GLAZE

1 tablespoon butter

1 shallot, minced

2 cloves garlic, minced

2 tablespoons ancho chile powder

¼ teaspoon red pepper flakes

½ cup honey

- Over medium heat, sauté shallot and garlic in butter until onion is soft.

- Add ancho chile powder and red pepper flakes.

- Mix in honey. Cook until slightly thickened. Strain.

SERVES 6

CILANTRO-LIME BUTTER

½ cup (1 stick) unsalted butter

1 shallot, minced

1 clove garlic, minced

2 tablespoons cilantro, minced

Juice of 1 lime

Salt and pepper to taste

- Melt butter. Add shallot and garlic; sauté until soft and butter smells nutty.

- Remove from heat and whisk in cilantro and lime juice.

- Salt and pepper to taste and serve immediately.

SERVES 6

JALAPEÑO CHEESE GRITS

2 jalapeños

3 tablespoons butter

½ cup onion, diced

1 clove garlic, minced

½ cup red bell pepper, diced

1 cup frozen corn

2 cups chicken broth

1 cup milk

1 cup heavy cream

Salt and pepper to taste

1 cup instant grits

2 eggs

2 cups Monterey Jack cheese, grated

- Preheat oven to 375°F.

- Slice jalapeños into thin circles and remove seeds and membrane. Reserve 8 slices for garnish.

- In 2 tablespoons of butter, sauté onion, garlic, jalapeño slices, red bell pepper, and corn until onion is soft.

- Add broth, milk, and cream. Bring to a boil; then simmer.

- Season with salt and pepper to taste. Slowly stir in grits and cook until thickened.

- Remove from heat and add eggs and cheese. Mix well.

- Pour into 2-quart Pyrex baking dish. Top with reserved jalapeno slices. Brush with 1 tablespoon melted butter and bake until golden, approximately 1 hour.

SERVES 6

SAUTÉED SUGAR SNAP PEAS

1 pound sugar snap peas, stringed

2 tablespoons butter

1 tablespoon lime juice

Salt and pepper to taste

- In salted boiling water, blanch sugar snap peas. Drain and place in cold water.

- Sauté in butter until hot. Add lime juice and salt and pepper to taste.

COWBOY CHOCOLATE CAKE

1½ sticks unsalted butter

3 cups sugar

3 large eggs

2 teaspoons vanilla

4 ounces unsweetened chocolate, melted

3 cups all-purpose flour

3 teaspoons baking soda

½ teaspoon salt

1 teaspoon cinnamon

¾ cup buttermilk

⅓ cup strong, boiling coffee

- Preheat oven to 325°F. Butter and flour 9x12-inch baking pan.

- Cream butter and sugar until light and fluffy. Add eggs and vanilla and beat until well blended.

- Add melted chocolate and beat 1 to 2 minutes.

- In separate bowl, combine flour, baking soda, salt, and cinnamon.

- Alternate adding dry mixture and buttermilk to butter and sugar mixture. Beat until blended.

- Slowly add boiling coffee and beat until smooth. Bake 1 hour.

- Serve with warm chocolate sauce.

WARM CHOCOLATE SAUCE

2 cups heavy cream

¼ teaspoon cayenne pepper

16 ounces semisweet chocolate

- Heat heavy cream until hot but not boiling. Remove from heat and add cayenne pepper and chocolate. Stir until blended.

PIN OAK STUD

FALL LUNCHEON

Sweet and Spicy Bacon Bits

Bibb Lettuce Salad

Tomato Soup with Lemon and Rosemary

Popovers

Chicken Divan

Apple Crisp

The history of Pin Oak Stud intertwines Kentucky and Texas lore. Oilman James S. Abercrombie's original Pin Oak Stable was established in Houston in 1938 and produced champion American Saddlebred Horses. In 1946 Abercrombie and his daughter, Josephine, formed a Thoroughbred syndicate and ventured to the yearling sales in Kentucky. This trip inspired them to acquire land in Woodford County, and that acreage also was christened Pin Oak.

Pin Oak Stud became a major farming operation, locally known for its Simmental cattle and its asparagus. After her parents' deaths, Josephine Abercrombie brought Pin Oak into a new realm. Among the top Thoroughbred horses bred at the farm was 1976 Preakness Stakes winner Elocutionist. Some years later Abercrombie purchased eight hundred acres nearby on Grassy Springs Road, where the English architect Quinlan Terry designed for her a Palladian country home. The barns and employee residences handsomely mirror the architecture of the main house. In late 1988 Abercrombie moved to this newly constructed Thoroughbred farm, built exclusively as a racing and breeding entity.

The 1990s brought Pin Oak an Eclipse Award for Laugh and Be Merry for best turf mare and Canadian Sovereign Awards for Horse of the Year Peaks and Valleys and champion grass horse Hasten To Add. Early in the twenty-first century the Pin Oak stallion Maria's Mon sired Kentucky Derby winner Monarchos.

Pin Oak was the Thoroughbred Owners and Breeders Association state and national Thoroughbred Breeder of the Year in 1995, becoming the first Kentucky breeder to win the national title.

SWEET AND SPICY BACON BITS

1 pound bacon, thick cut

1¼ cups brown sugar

1 tablespoon cinnamon

⅛ teaspoon cayenne

⅛ teaspoon ground coriander

1 tablespoon sesame seeds

- Preheat oven to 375°F.
- Line baking sheet with parchment paper.
- Cut bacon strips into 3 pieces each.
- Combine next 4 ingredients and coat each piece of bacon.
- Place bacon on parchment paper and bake for 10 minutes. Take out and sprinkle lightly with sesame seeds and return to oven for 5 to 10 minutes until bacon is sizzling and brown.
- Transfer to paper towels to drain.

MAKES APPROXIMATELY 36 PIECES

BIBB LETTUCE SALAD

½ teaspoon onion, diced

½ cup sugar

½ teaspoon fresh garlic, diced

1 tablespoon salt

1 tablespoon paprika

1 tablespoon Worcestershire sauce

1 tablespoon dried mustard

½ teaspoon black pepper

¼ teaspoon ground red pepper

⅔ cup vinegar

1 (10-ounce) can tomato soup

⅔ cup canola or vegetable oil

4 heads fresh Bibb lettuce, rinsed and dried

- Combine all ingredients for dressing and refrigerate until chilled.
- Serve over Bibb lettuce.

SERVES 6 TO 8

TOMATO SOUP WITH LEMON AND ROSEMARY

4 tablespoons (½ stick) butter

1 onion, finely chopped

2 carrots, peeled, finely chopped

3 cloves garlic, peeled and chopped

½ teaspoon dried thyme

½ teaspoon dried crushed red pepper

1 bay leaf

Salt and pepper

2 (28-ounce) cans crushed tomatoes (with added purée)

6 cups chicken broth

½ cup half & half or heavy cream

¾ teaspoon fresh rosemary, minced

2 teaspoons grated lemon zest

- In large soup pot, melt butter and add next 6 ingredients. Cover and cook for 5 minutes over medium heat, stirring occasionally.
- Add tomatoes and broth. Cover and simmer for 40 minutes.
- Discard bay leaf and adjust seasonings with salt and pepper.
- In separate bowl, whisk cream, rosemary, and ½ teaspoon lemon zest.
- Stir remaining lemon zest into soup.
- To serve, ladle soup into bowls and drizzle the cream and rosemary mixture over top.

SERVES 8

POPOVERS

1 cup sifted all-purpose flour

¼ teaspoon salt

¾ cup plus 2 tablespoons milk

2 eggs, well beaten

1 tablespoon unsalted butter,
   melted

- Preheat oven to 425°F.
- Sift together flour and salt.
- Gradually stir in milk and beat until mixture is smooth.
- Add eggs and butter.
- Beat for 2 minutes. (Do not overbeat.)
- Grease muffin or popover tins generously with butter. Fill tins
  ⅔ full with batter.
- Bake for 15 minutes at 425°F. Turn oven temperature down to
  350°F and bake 15 to 20 minutes longer. Serve immediately.

MAKES 8 POPOVERS

CHICKEN DIVAN

⅓ cup butter

6 tablespoons all-purpose flour

1 cup chicken stock

1 cup light cream

2 egg yolks

Hot sauce to taste

½ cup sherry

2 teaspoons fresh lemon juice

1½ pounds fresh broccoli florets,
   steamed

1¼ pounds chicken breasts, cooked

1 cup freshly grated
   Parmesan cheese

Salt and pepper to taste

- Preheat oven to 350°F.
- Melt butter over low heat.
- Add flour and whisk until well blended.
- Remove from heat and blend in chicken stock and cream.
- Return to heat and cook, stirring constantly until thick and smooth.
- Beat egg yolks well, adding a little hot sauce to yolks while stirring.
- Pour small amount of chicken stock mixture into eggs to temper.
- Pour eggs back into main chicken stock mixture.
- Add sherry and lemon juice.
- Arrange cooked broccoli in shallow baking dish and cover with
  cooked chicken breasts.
- Pour sauce over chicken and broccoli. Bake 40 minutes, then sprinkle
  with Parmesan cheese. Continue cooking until lightly browned and
  bubbling.

SERVES 8 TO 10

APPLE CRISP

8–10 apples, peeled, cored,
   and sliced

6 teaspoons lemon juice

1½ cups brown sugar,
   firmly packed

1 teaspoon ground cinnamon

1¼ cups dry oatmeal
   (regular or quick cooking)

¾ cup unsalted butter

- Preheat oven to 400°F.
- Layer apples in 7x11-inch buttered baking dish. Sprinkle with lemon
  juice.
- Combine brown sugar, cinnamon, and oatmeal in bowl.
- Cut in butter until mixture has a crumbly consistency and sprinkle
  over apples.
- Bake 45 minutes or until apples are tender. Serve warm with
  ice cream or whipped cream.

SERVES 6 TO 8

RUNNYMEDE FARM

FALL HUNT DINNER

Butternut Squash Soup

Favorite Greens with Rosemary Vinaigrette Dressing

Peas with Fresh Spinach

Doves à la Spears

Wild Rice Casserole

Buttermilk Biscuits

Amelia's Field Warm Chocolate Pudding Cake

Recognized as the oldest Thoroughbred farm in Kentucky continuously owned by one family, Runnymede Farm was established in 1867 by Colonel Ezekiel F. Clay and his brother-in-law Colonel Catesby Woodford. Some of the buildings on the farm, located outside Paris, date from even earlier times. The stone barn was built in 1803 as Cooper's Run Baptist Church. The residence at Runnymede was built in the 1830s.

During the early decades of its operation, when post-Civil War racing blossomed, Runnymede emerged as an important source of high-class racehorses. The farm bred Hanover, a champion who won twenty of twenty-seven races as a three-year-old and went on to be the leading stallion in America for four consecutive seasons. Also foaled at Runnymede during that era was the redoubtable Miss Woodford, who became the first horse to earn $100,000 racing in America. Such horses are among the Runnymede champions portrayed by a noted artist of the day, Henry Stull, whose paintings grace the farm residence.

Catesby W. Clay, a grandson of Colonel Clay, is at the farm's helm today. Under Catesby Clay's leadership, Runnymede has enjoyed international influence. Successful Runnymede-bred horses have included Japan's Horse of the Year Agnes Digital and Full Extent, winner of England's Gimcrack Stakes.

In this country Runnymede has bred Kentucky Derby runner-up Tejano Run, the outstanding mare Plankton, and Angle Light (the only three-year-old to defeat Secretariat). In the early 2000s Runnymede was represented by such top horses as Withers Stakes winner Divine Park and England's Racing Post Trophy winner Palace Episode.

BUTTERNUT SQUASH SOUP

6 pounds butternut squash, peeled, seeded, and chopped

1 pound potatoes, peeled and chopped

½ pound prosciutto, de-fatted and diced ½-inch thick

12 shallots, sliced ¼-inch thick

1½ tablespoons salt

2 pints heavy cream

2 Granny Smith apples, cored and finely diced

2 bunches cilantro, chopped into thin strips

2 red bell peppers, seeded and diced

Salt and pepper to taste

- Combine squash, potatoes, prosciutto, shallots, and salt in a large pot. Add enough water to almost cover, as squash will render additional liquid.

- Boil until potatoes and squash are just done (vegetables should not get mushy).

- Put mixture into blender in batches. Blend each batch to a fine purée on a high speed and strain through a very fine sieve into a medium saucepan.

- Add cream and return mixture to a simmer. Season to taste with salt and pepper.

- In a separate bowl, combine apple, cilantro, and red pepper.

- To serve, ladle soup into bowls and garnish with apple mixture.

SERVES 8 TO 10

FAVORITE GREENS WITH ROSEMARY VINAIGRETTE DRESSING

ROSEMARY VINAIGRETTE

1 tablespoon onions, chopped

½ cup honey

3 tablespoons Dijon mustard

1 cup balsamic vinegar

1 tablespoon fresh rosemary, chopped

4 cloves garlic, chopped

1 teaspoon hot sauce

1 tablespoon soy sauce

Salt and pepper

3 cups olive oil

- Combine all ingredients except olive oil.

- Using a wire whisk, slowly add olive oil until all is incorporated. Keep dressing refrigerated.

- Serve over a combination of favorite lettuce greens.

MAKES APPROXIMATELY 4½ CUPS DRESSING

PEAS WITH FRESH SPINACH

2 (16-ounce) bags frozen
petite peas, rinsed and drained

¾ cup water

3 tablespoons butter

Sea salt and freshly ground
black pepper to taste

2 cups fresh baby spinach

- Place the peas in medium saucepan with ¾ cup water, 1 tablespoon butter, salt, and pepper and bring to a low boil. When peas have reached a bright green color (3 to 4 minutes), remove from heat and drain.

- Place peas in saucepan with remaining 2 tablespoons butter.

- Add spinach and heat until spinach has begun to wilt. The peas and spinach should still have a fresh green color when served.

SERVES 8

DOVES À LA SPEARS

16 doves, dressed

1½ cups flour

Salt and pepper

3 bouillon cubes

3 cups hot water

3 tablespoons unsalted butter

- Preheat oven to 300°F.

- Roll doves in flour, salt, and pepper. Shake off excess flour.

- Dissolve bouillon cubes in the 3 cups of hot water and set aside.

- Melt 3 tablespoons of butter in skillet. Brown doves on both sides, adding more butter as needed to brown all birds.

- Place browned doves in a casserole dish (make sure dish has a cover). Pour bouillon over doves.

- Cover casserole dish and bake at 300°F for 2 hours or until birds are tender.

SERVES 8

WILD RICE CASSEROLE

1 cup wild rice, soaked overnight

1 (10.5-ounce) can consommé, undiluted

4 tablespoons butter

¾ pound fresh mushrooms, sliced

6–8 scallions, sliced

1½ cups finely chopped celery

1 (6-ounce) can water chestnuts, drained and sliced

½ cup vermouth

- Wash and drain soaked rice and combine with consommé in a large saucepan.

- Simmer rice, covered, for about 30 minutes or until liquid is absorbed.

- Melt butter in a skillet and sauté mushrooms, onions, and celery until limp.

- Add vegetables and water chestnuts to rice and combine. Put in a buttered 2-quart casserole. Refrigerate until ready to use.

- When ready to bake, add vermouth and dot top with butter. Bake at 350°F for 30 to 40 minutes.

SERVES 8

BUTTERMILK BISCUITS

2 cups unbleached all-purpose flour

1 tablespoon baking powder

¼ teaspoon baking soda

½ teaspoon salt

1 tablespoon sugar

⅓ cup vegetable shortening

1 cup buttermilk

- Preheat the over to 450°F.

- Sift the flour, baking powder, baking soda, salt, and sugar into a medium bowl.

- Using a pastry cutter or your fingers, cut in the shortening until the mixture resembles coarse crumbs. Add the buttermilk. Stir quickly until the dough is soft and follows the fork around the bowl.

- Turn out onto a lightly floured surface and knead gently for 10 to 12 seconds, adding flour as necessary.

- Roll the dough until it is ½-inch thick. With a floured biscuit cutter, cut straight down into the dough.

- Place biscuits 1 inch apart on an ungreased baking sheet. Bake for 12 to 15 minutes, until light golden brown.

MAKES 12 TO 14 BISCUITS

AMELIA'S FIELD WARM CHOCOLATE PUDDING CAKE

6 ounces good-quality semisweet chocolate, finely chopped

2 ounces unsweetened chocolate, finely chopped

12 tablespoons plus 3 teaspoons unsalted butter, softened

¾ cup sugar

4 large eggs

¾ cup all-purpose flour

1 teaspoon baking powder

2 tablespoons unsweetened cocoa powder

Whipped cream for garnish

Cocoa powder for garnish

- Lightly butter 8 ramekins with 3 teaspoons butter and set aside.

- In the top of a double boiler, place semisweet and unsweetened chocolate and stir occasionally until melted.

- Remove double boiler. After incorporating ¾ cup butter and sugar, pour this mixture into a mixing bowl; then add eggs, flour, baking powder, and cocoa.

- With an electric mixer, beat at medium-high speed until mixture is pale and very thick, about 7 minutes. Place mixture in prepared ramekins, filling about half-full.

- Cover with plastic wrap and freeze for at least 3 hours.

- When ready to serve, preheat oven to 375°F.

- Place ramekins on a baking sheet and set on the middle shelf in the oven and bake until edges are browned.

- Invert pudding cakes onto plates and serve immediately, garnished with whipped cream or ice cream, and dusted with cocoa powder. Desserts may be served directly from ramekins.

SERVES 8

SHAWNEE FARM

FALL SUPPER

Shrimp in Dijon Vinaigrette

Curried Pineapple Rice

Steamed Broccoli with Oriental Hollandaise Sauce

Balsamic-Soy Rack of Lamb

Alabama Biscuits

Raspberry-White Chocolate Cheesecake

Two Kentucky Derby winners, Leonatus and Genuine Risk, are associated with Shawnee Farm, though in very different eras.

In the nineteenth century, Colonel Jack Chinn, owned part of the property and raced in partnership 1883 Kentucky Derby winner Leonatus. A few years later Chinn called the place Leonatus Farm. His son, raconteur Colonel Phil Chinn, was born there in 1874 and grew up believing the farm's spring generated "the best drinking water in the world."

In 1939 Mrs. Parker Poe acquired the property and was more interested in Jersey cattle, hunter show horses, and foxhounds than in Thoroughbreds. However, Poe did convert to breeding Thoroughbreds, and during her tenure Shawnee, named for the creek it abuts, became the birthplace of twenty-six added money winners, one of them being champion race mare Bornastar.

Poe's great-nephew G. Watts Humphrey Jr. and his wife, Sally, purchased the property, which covers more than a thousand acres in Mercer County, outside Harrodsburg, in 1978. Its distinctive green fencing blends especially well with the fields of bluegrass.

Under the Humphreys' guidance, Shawnee Farm has remained a source of many outstanding horses, including champions Misil, Sacahuista, Clear Mandate, and Genuine Risk, who in 1980 was only the second filly in history to win the Kentucky Derby. Humphrey, in a partnership with his aunt Pamela Firman, also bred Crème Fraiche, who went on to win the Belmont Stakes in 1985.

SHRIMP IN DIJON VINAIGRETTE

½ cup finely chopped fresh parsley

½ cup finely chopped shallots

½ cup tarragon vinegar

½ cup white wine vinegar

1 cup olive oil

8 tablespoons Dijon mustard

4 teaspoons red pepper flakes

2 teaspoons ground black pepper

1 tablespoon fresh lemon juice

3 pounds large shrimp, cooked, peeled, and deveined

- Combine parsley and remaining ingredients and pour over warm shrimp.
- Toss well so that every shrimp is coated with mixture.
- Cover and refrigerate for at least 8 to 10 hours.
- Drain excess marinade from shrimp before serving.
- Serve in a bowl lined with lettuce or on salad plates with shredded lettuce for a first course.

SERVES 8 TO 10

CURRIED PINEAPPLE RICE

3 tablespoons unsalted butter

1 tablespoon fresh ginger, finely minced

1½ cups long grain white rice, drained and rinsed (not instant or converted)

½ cup raisins

⅓ cup slivered almonds, toasted

⅓ cup red bell pepper, minced

½ cup scallions, minced

1 cup fresh pineapple, diced

SAUCE

2¼ cups chicken broth

1 tablespoon curry powder

¼ cup unsweetened coconut milk

½ teaspoon Chinese chili sauce

2 tablespoons light soy sauce

½ teaspoon salt

2 tablespoons lime juice

½ teaspoon minced lime zest

- Place a 3-quart saucepan over medium heat. Add butter and ginger. Sauté until butter sizzles; then add rice.
- Stir rice until coated with butter and well heated, about 5 minutes.
- Combine sauce ingredients.
- Add raisins and sauce to rice mixture.
- Bring to low boil, stirring, and then cover; reduce heat to lowest setting, and simmer until all liquid is absorbed, about 18 to 24 minutes.
- Remove cover and stir in almonds, red bell pepper, scallions, and pineapple. Serve immediately.

SERVES 6 TO 8

STEAMED BROCCOLI WITH ORIENTAL HOLLANDAISE SAUCE

1 bunch broccoli

3 large egg yolks

2 tablespoons lemon juice

1 tablespoon unsalted butter
at room temperature

7 tablespoons unsalted butter,
hot and melted

¼ teaspoon salt

¼ teaspoon ground Sichuan
peppercorns

¼ teaspoon white pepper

1 teaspoon fresh ginger, minced

1 teaspoon lemon zest, grated

- Steam broccoli florets until bright green and tender.

- To make sauce: In small double boiler, beat egg yolks and half of lemon juice.

- Add tablespoon of room temperature butter.

- Bring water in double boiler to simmer and beat egg yolks with a whisk until sauce thickens to consistency of heavy cream.

- Remove from heat and very slowly beat in hot melted butter.

- Stir in rest of ingredients and pour over broccoli.

SERVES 6 TO 8

BALSAMIC-SOY RACK OF LAMB

2 racks of lamb

2 tablespoons mixed red, green,
and white peppercorns

½ cup honey

¼ cup Dijon mustard

BALSAMIC-SOY MARINADE

¾ cup balsamic vinegar

¾ cup dry white wine

½ cup dark soy sauce

10 cloves garlic, finely minced

- With knife, make small cut along backbone between each of the ribs so meat is slightly pierced.

- Place lamb in non-reactive container.

- Place peppercorns in sauté pan over medium heat and toast until peppercorns begin to pop and hop. Transfer to spice grinder or mortar and coarsely grind.

- Combine honey and mustard and set aside.

- In small container, combine vinegar, wine, soy sauce, and garlic. Pour over lamb.

- Cover and refrigerate for at least 2 to 8 hours.

- One hour prior to cooking, remove lamb from refrigerator. Rub lamb with pepper mix; then rub it with honey mustard.

- Prepare grill to medium heat and grill lamb for 17 to 20 minutes or until meat thermometer reaches internal temperature of 140°F (medium rare). (To roast in oven, preheat oven to 450°F. Roast the lamb for about 20 minutes for medium rare.)

- Allow lamb to sit for 5 to 10 minutes before serving.

SERVES 6 TO 8

ALABAMA BISCUITS

2½ cups all-purpose flour, plus a little more for rolling out

4 tablespoons sugar

½ teaspoon baking soda

½ teaspoon salt

6 tablespoons vegetable shortening

1 package yeast

1 cup buttermilk at room temperature

½ cup (1 stick) unsalted butter, melted

- Preheat oven to 400°F.

- Sift first four ingredients.

- With pastry cutter or two knives, cut in shortening.

- Dissolve yeast in cup of buttermilk.

- Pour buttermilk mixture into dry ingredients.

- Mix and turn dough onto floured surface. Knead dough about 30 times.

- Roll dough out to ¼-inch thickness.

- Cut out biscuits with a 2-inch biscuit cutter. Brush each biscuit with melted butter; then place one biscuit on top of another. Brush top of double-tiered biscuits with remaining butter.

- Allow to rise in warm place, covered loosely with wax paper and out of drafts for at least one hour.

- Bake at 400°F for 20 minutes or until done.

MAKES APPROXIMATELY 18 TO 20 BISCUITS

RASPBERRY-WHITE CHOCOLATE CHEESECAKE

CRUST

1 (9-ounce) package chocolate wafers, coarsely broken up

6 tablespoons unsalted butter, melted

FILLING

12 ounces frozen unsweetened raspberries, thawed, juice reserved

6 ounces good-quality white chocolate

4 (8-ounce) packages cream cheese, at room temperature

1½ cups sugar

2 tablespoons all-purpose flour

4 large eggs

2 tablespoons whipping cream

2 teaspoons vanilla

½ teaspoon almond extract

- Preheat oven to 325°F.

- Double wrap with heavy foil the sides and bottom of a 9-inch springform pan.

- Place cookies in food processor and pulse until coarse crumbs form.

- Add butter and process until moistened.

- Press into bottom of pan and bake for 8 minutes.

- Press raspberries and juice through a sieve into a small bowl.

- Measure ½ cup of raspberry purée for filling.

- In a double boiler, heat white chocolate over barely simmering water until just melted. Set aside.

- In a large bowl, beat cream cheese and sugar with an electric mixer until mixture is smooth and fluffy.

- Beat in flour; then add eggs one at a time. Beat in whipping cream and vanilla.

- Transfer 2½ cups of batter to a medium-sized bowl. Stir in melted chocolate.

- Add reserved ½ cup raspberry purée and almond extract into remaining batter in large bowl.

- Pour raspberry batter over crust.

- To make a water bath, place foil-wrapped springform pan in a large baking pan with deep sides. Pour enough hot water to reach 1 inch up the sides of the pan. Bake at 325°F until raspberry filling is softly set in center and beginning to puff at edges, about 50 minutes. Cool for 5 minutes to let cake firm slightly.

- Starting at edge of pan, spoon white chocolate batter in concentric circles onto raspberry filling and smooth top. Bake at 325°F until white chocolate filling is set, about 30 minutes. Refrigerate cheesecake at least 4 hours, uncovered. To serve, gently remove the sides of the springform pan, slice cake into pieces, and using a spatula, remove individual slice of cake onto dessert plate.

- Garnish with white chocolate curls and fresh raspberries.

SERVES 8 TO 10

STONE FARM

SUNDAY NIGHT CHILI SUPPER

Hot Reuben Dip

Blue Cole Slaw

Fireside Venison Chili

Scallion Cornmeal Fritters

Cranberry Gingerbread with Brown Sugar Whipped Cream

Fourth-generation horseman Arthur Hancock III has followed a long family history while also making his own mark. As a member of the Hancock family of Claiborne Farm, Hancock grew up steeped in the lore of the Turf. His great-grandfather had launched the family breeding enterprise in Virginia, and his grandfather and father had guided Claiborne Farm to international acclaim.

At his own Stone Farm, Hancock has followed his ancestors' example of high standards. He and his wife, Staci, also are involved with charitable causes connected to equine welfare, including the Kentucky Equine Humane Center. The Hancocks set a splendid example by repurchasing Kentucky Derby winner Gato Del Sol to provide him a comfortable home in his old age.

In 1982 Gato Del Sol became the first Kentucky Derby winner for Stone Farm and for the Hancock family. He was bred and raced by Hancock in partnership with Leone J. Peters. Next came Sunday Silence, who in 1989 won the Derby, the Preakness, and the Breeders' Cup Classic en route to being named Horse of the Year. Afer being sold to Japan for stud duty, Sunday Silence became a public icon as well as an international stallion. Hancock also has a passion for country music as a singer and song writer.

In partnership with Stonerside Stable's Robert McNair, Hancock bred Fusaichi Pegasus. Sold for $4 million as a yearling, Fusaichi Pegasus won the Kentucky Derby in 2000. Hancock's other important victories have included the 1988 Kentucky Oaks with Goodbye Halo, owned in partnership with friend and fellow Kentuckian Alex Campbell.

HOT REUBEN DIP

1 (8-ounce) package cream cheese, softened

½ cup sour cream

2 tablespoons ketchup

½ pound corned beef, finely chopped

1 cup sauerkraut, drained

4 ounces Swiss cheese, shredded

2 tablespoons onion, finely chopped

- Mix cream cheese, sour cream, and ketchup until smooth. Stir in remaining ingredients until well blended. Transfer to 1-quart baking dish.

- Bake covered at 375°F for 25 minutes; then bake uncovered for another 5 minutes. Serve with rye Triscuits.

MAKES APPROXIMATELY 4 CUPS

BLUE COLE SLAW

8 ounces blue cheese crumbles

2 bags (8 cups) of cole slaw mix

1 cup vegetable oil

2 cloves garlic, minced

½ teaspoon black pepper

½ teaspoon salt

¼ teaspoon dry mustard

1 teaspoon celery seed

2 teaspoons sugar

½ cup minced onion

½ cup apple cider vinegar

- Combine blue cheese crumbles and slaw mix and set aside.

- Combine the rest of the ingredients. Pour over the slaw, toss, and chill.

- For another twist, add freshly chopped dill when available.

SERVES 8

FIRESIDE VENISON CHILI

1 cup red or white wine

1 tablespoon salt

1 tablespoon black pepper

9 cups cubed venison (tenderloin, steak, rib, etc., or combination thereof)

2 tablespoons olive oil

2 tablespoons chili powder (the hotter the better!)

1 tablespoon cumin

1 tablespoon cinnamon

1–2 tablespoons dried, crushed red pepper flakes

2 red bell peppers (4–5 cups), chopped

2 yellow onions (4–5 cups), chopped

2 (15-ounce) cans kidney beans, drained (or any other bean you prefer)

1 (15-ounce) can white sweet corn, drained

1 (15-ounce) can small black olives, drained

2 (15-ounce) cans crushed tomatoes

2 (15-ounce) cans petite diced tomatoes

1 (7.5-ounce) can jalapeños

Pasta or rice for 8

Grated cheddar cheese

Hot sauce

- In large mixing bowl, stir wine, salt, and black pepper together. Add meat to mixture and put in a large resealable plastic bag. Marinate in refrigerator for about 24 hours.

- When you are ready to make chili, heat oil to sizzle in large heavy pot. Whisk in spices (chili powder, cumin, cinnamon, red pepper flakes). Quickly add entire bag of meat and marinade. Brown meat over medium heat until done. Stir in remaining ingredients and simmer on low heat for about 1 hour.

- Serve over pasta or rice. Top with grated cheese (sharp cheddar is preferred). Serve hot sauce on side.

(Note: If venison is not available, mix meats for another version: 3 cups of pork, 3 cups of chicken, 3 cups of beef. The variation of flavor and texture is interesting.)

SERVES 8

CRANBERRY GINGERBREAD WITH BROWN SUGAR WHIPPED CREAM

3 cups all-purpose flour

1½ teaspoons baking powder

1½ teaspoons ground cinnamon

1½ teaspoons ground ginger

¾ teaspoon baking soda

¾ teaspoon salt

¾ teaspoon ground allspice

¼ teaspoon ground cloves

¾ cup unsalted butter, at room temperature

¾ cup firmly packed dark brown sugar

2 large eggs

1 cup plus 2 tablespoons unsulfured light molasses

1 cup plus 2 tablespoons buttermilk

2½ cups fresh cranberries, coarsely chopped in food processor

⅓ cup chopped crystallized ginger

Additional ground cinnamon

- Preheat oven to 350°F. Grease 13x9x2-inch glass baking dish; dust with flour.

- Sift first 8 ingredients into medium bowl.

- Using electric mixer, beat butter in separate mixing bowl and add brown sugar until mixture is light and fluffy. Add eggs one at a time, beating well after each addition. Pour in molasses and beat to combine.

- Add dry ingredients alternately with buttermilk into egg mixture, beginning and ending with dry ingredients. Fold in cranberries and crystallized ginger.

- Spread batter in prepared pan. Bake at 350°F until springy to touch, about 50 minutes. Cool cake in pan on wire rack.

- Serve warm or at room temperature with brown sugar whipped cream and a sprinkling of cinnamon. (recipe at right)

SERVES 8 TO 12

SCALLION CORNMEAL FRITTERS

1 large egg, slightly beaten

1 cup whole milk

1⅓ cups yellow cornmeal
(stone-ground preferred)

1 teaspoon baking powder

½ teaspoon salt

2 tablespoons finely chopped
scallion greens

½ cup or more vegetable oil

* Put oven rack in middle position. Preheat oven to 200°F.

* Whisk together egg, milk, cornmeal, baking powder, salt, and scallion greens in bowl until combined.

* Heat a ½-inch of oil in a 10-inch heavy skillet over moderately high heat until oil is hot but not smoking.

* Fill ¼-cup measure half full with batter and carefully spoon it into the skillet. Form 4 more fritters in the skillet and fry, turning over once, until golden, 3 to 4 minutes total.

* Transfer fritters to paper towels to drain briefly. To keep the fritters warm, arrange them in single layer in shallow baking pan in oven. Make more fritters in same manner. Do not crowd skillet.

MAKES 18 FRITTERS

BROWN SUGAR WHIPPED CREAM

1 cup chilled whipping cream

⅓ cup chilled sour cream

⅓ cup packed dark brown sugar

1½ teaspoons vanilla extract

* With electric mixer, beat whipping cream until stiff peaks form.

* Add rest of ingredients to whipped cream and beat until incorporated. Can be prepared up to 4 hours ahead. Cover and refrigerate.

MAKES ABOUT 2⅔ CUPS

STONERSIDE

A FALL GAME SUPPER

Tortilla Chips and Black Bean Salsa

Spicy Shrimp

Grilled Marinated Doves

Chicken Enchiladas

Hunter's Favorite Cookie

In 1995 Texas residents Janice and Robert McNair purchased 1,250 acres in Bourbon County adjacent to two of the most historic horse farms of Kentucky, Stone Farm and Stoner Creek Stud. Demonstrating an appreciation for their new surroundings and history, the McNairs quickly created their own addition to the landscape, commissioning a covered bridge that is believed to be the first such structure built in Kentucky in 120 years. At 200 feet long, the triple-span wood bridge rises more than twenty-six feet above Stoner Creek. The main home on the farm dates back to the late eighteenth century; an old schoolhouse on the property has been converted into another residence.

The McNairs entered racing at the top levels, just as Robert McNair later did when investing in an NFL team, the Houston Texans. The couple's first purchase, Southern Truce, won a graded stakes in her first start for the McNairs. Further success for Stonerside came with the purchase of future champion Chilukki, and with homebred Congaree, a five-time grade I winner of more than $3 million. The McNairs had great luck in a partnership with Arthur B. Hancock III (Stone Farm), with whom they co-owned 1994 Kentucky Derby runner-up Strodes Creek, and co-bred 2000 Kentucky Derby winner Fusaichi Pegasus and grade II winner E Dubai.

Stonerside, now encompassing 1,947 acres, had raced fifty-five stakes winners through mid-2007, including eight millionaires. Although most homebreds are raced, the farm has had an impact at public auction, selling Blue Grass Stakes winner The Cliff's Edge and group II winner and successful young sire Van Nistelrooy. Stonerside achieved another milestone in 2005 by becoming the first farm to sell three yearlings for $3 million or more in a single year.

BLACK BEAN SALSA

MARINADE:

5 tablespoons extra virgin olive oil

2½ tablespoons red wine vinegar

5 tablespoons fresh lime juice

2½ teaspoons sea salt

2½ teaspoons freshly ground
black pepper

SALSA:

2 (15-ounce) cans black beans,
rinsed and drained

5 ears of corn, cooked and cut
from cob

1 medium red onion, chopped

3 large tomatoes, peeled, seeded,
and chopped

2 fresh jalapeño peppers, seeded
and minced

2 avocados

Fresh flat-leaf parsley and/or
cilantro for garnish

- Whisk together all marinade ingredients. Set aside.

- Combine salsa ingredients, except avocados. Toss lightly.

- Pour marinade over salsa. Cover and refrigerate for at least 1 hour.

- Peel and chop avocados and add to salsa. Toss gently again and garnish with flat-leaf parsley and/or cilantro. Serve with tortilla chips.

MAKES APPROXIMATELY 7 CUPS

SPICY SHRIMP

½ cup (1 stick) unsalted butter

4–5 pounds of large shrimp,
peeled and deveined

2 limes

Garlic salt to taste

1 (7-ounce) can chipotle peppers
(ready to eat), puréed

½ teaspoon cumin

4 cups sour cream

Chopped fresh cilantro for garnish

- Melt butter in large skillet and add shrimp in batches. Squeeze juice from limes over shrimp and add garlic salt to taste.

- Sauté shrimp until cooked through. Drain shrimp.

- In mixing bowl, combine puréed peppers, cumin, and sour cream. Add to shrimp and cook until heated through.

- Serve topped with cilantro

SERVES 12 TO 15 AS APPETIZER

GRILLED MARINATED DOVES

38–40 dove breast fillets

1 (16-ounce) bottle zesty
Italian dressing

1 teaspoon red pepper flakes

10 jalapeño peppers

20 slices of bacon

- Place breast fillets in non-reactive pan. Cover with Italian dressing and red pepper flakes and marinate in refrigerator at least 6 hours.

- Quarter each jalapeño pepper and remove seeds. Cut bacon strips into big enough pieces to wrap around each fillet.

- When ready to prepare, discard the marinade, place a piece of jalapeno on dove fillet, and wrap with bacon. Secure with toothpick. Grill at medium heat until done, 7 to 9 minutes.

SERVES 20

CHICKEN ENCHILADAS

2 tablespoons olive oil

8 boneless, skinless chicken breasts, diced

Salt and pepper

2 cloves garlic, minced

Juice of 1 lime

2 (8-ounce) packages cream cheese, softened

2 medium onions, chopped

2 jalapeño peppers, diced

2 teaspoons salt

2 teaspoons pepper

3 teaspoons garlic powder

2 (14-ounce) cans chopped tomatoes (do not drain)

2 (4-ounce) cans chopped green chiles

3 teaspoons ground cumin

2 teaspoons coriander

2 teaspoons ground curry powder

6–8 dashes hot pepper sauce

2 cups sour cream

16 large flour tortillas

2 cups Monterey Jack cheese, shredded

4 cups mozzarella cheese, shredded

Toppings: chopped lettuce, sour cream, diced tomatoes

- Preheat oven to 375°F.

- Heat olive oil in large skillet and add diced chicken. Sprinkle with salt, pepper, and minced garlic. Squeeze juice of 1 lime onto chicken. Cook until chicken is done. Transfer to large bowl.

- Add cream cheese, onion, jalapeño, and 1 teaspoon each of salt and pepper, and 2 teaspoons garlic powder to the cooked chicken. Combine ingredients well and set aside.

- In blender, add tomatoes with juice; chiles; cumin; coriander; curry powder; remaining garlic powder, salt, and pepper; and 6 to 8 dashes of hot pepper sauce. Blend until smooth. Add sour cream and blend until incorporated.

- Spray two 9x13-inch pans with cooking spray. Place tortillas on clean work surface and fill with about ¼ cup chicken mixture; roll into a cylinder and place in prepared pans. Pour sauce over tortillas. Cover pans with foil and bake 45 minutes.

- Remove foil; cover with cheeses and bake additional 5 to 10 minutes or until cheese is melted. Top with lettuce, tomatoes, and sour cream.

SERVES 20

HUNTER'S FAVORITE COOKIE

1½ cups honey graham cracker crumbs

½ cup all-purpose flour

¼ teaspoon baking powder

1 (14-ounce) can sweetened condensed milk

½ cup margarine, softened

1 can flaked coconut

1¼ cups chocolate chips

1 cup peanut butter morsels

1 cup chopped walnuts or pecans

- Preheat oven to 375°F.

- Mix cracker crumbs, flour, and baking powder in bowl. In large mixing bowl, beat condensed milk and margarine until smooth. Add cracker-crumb mixture and mix well. Stir in coconut, chocolate chips, peanut butter morsels, and nuts.

- Drop by rounded tablespoonfuls onto ungreased cookie sheet.

- Bake 9 to 10 minutes, or until lightly browned.

MAKES 2 TO 2½ DOZEN COOKIES

WINSTAR FARM

MEN'S FALL LUNCHEON

Hot Cheese with Pita Chips

Goat Cheese Salad with Pancetta, Dried Cherry, and Port Dressing

Roasted Garlic and Balsamic Vinegar Dipping Oil

Roasted Brussels Sprouts and Carrots

Pork Wellington

Grenoble Tart

Nature's beauty greets visitors to WinStar Farm before they even reach the farm proper. Along Pisgah Pike, rows of Osage-orange trees line and arch across the roadway. The farm itself carries on a comparable theme of lushness, with the vine-covered fronts of some of the barns, creating coolness in summer as well as beauty.

WinStar's owners, Kenny Troutt and Bill Casner, added to the land they purchased as Prestonwood Farm, with the property growing to more than 1,400 acres. The core of the farm was known as Silver Pond Farm after the Williams family of Virginia settled the land in the 1700s. The original farmhouse, smoke house, pond, and some of the barns are on the National Register of Historic Places, as is that alley of Osage-orange trees.

While respectful of the past, the current owners are cutting edge in their care of horses and in the construction of well-appointed offices and barns. Troutt and Casner were among the first breeders to invest in a hyperbaric chamber, an elaborate experiment in oxygen enhancement with healing properties. After acquisition of the farm, the owners quickly became enmeshed in leadership in the industry, with Casner serving as head of the Thoroughbred Owners and Breeders Association while also developing and supporting several of the industry's charities.

Some of the roadways on the farm are named for horses with WinStar connections, including Funny Cide. The 2003 Kentucky Derby and Preakness winner was foaled in New York, but sired by one of WinStar's stallions, Distorted Humor. Another distinguished WinStar stallion, Tiznow, offers the distinction of being the only two-time winner of the Breeders' Cup Classic.

HOT CHEESE

1 medium onion, grated

1 (4-ounce) jar pimentos and juice

1½ pounds sharp cheddar cheese, grated

1 pint mayonnaise

1–2 tablespoons Tabasco sauce

1 teaspoon garlic powder

- Put onion and pimentos with juice in food processor and purée.

- Combine cheese, mayonnaise, Tabasco sauce, and garlic powder. Add to the puréed mixture in food processor and pulse until all ingredients are combined.

- Store in refrigerator in sealed containers. Serve with pita chips or bread sticks.

MAKES 3 PINTS

ROASTED GARLIC AND BALSAMIC VINEGAR DIPPING OIL

25 cloves garlic, unpeeled

2 tablespoons plus 1 cup extra virgin olive oil

Salt and pepper to taste

½ cup balsamic vinegar

2½ teaspoons fresh rosemary, minced

- Preheat oven to 350°F.

- Place unpeeled garlic cloves in baking dish and add 2 tablespoons olive oil. Sprinkle with salt and pepper; toss to coat. Cover dish tightly with foil and bake until garlic is golden brown and tender, approximately 45 minutes. Allow to cool.

- Squeeze garlic between fingertips to release cloves. Transfer garlic cloves to blender. Add vinegar and rosemary and purée until smooth.

- With the machine still running, slowly add the remaining 1 cup of olive oil. Season to taste with salt and pepper. (Note: Dipping oil can be prepared one day ahead. Cover and refrigerate. Allow to stand 15 minutes at room temperature and whisk before using.) Serve with a baguette of French bread.

SERVES 6 TO 8 FOR DIPPING

ROASTED BRUSSELS SPROUTS AND CARROTS

1½ pounds Brussels sprouts (washed, ends cut off, outer leaves removed)

12 carrots, sliced diagonally into 1½-inch to 2-inch slices

4–6 tablespoons extra virgin olive oil

2 teaspoons kosher salt

1 teaspoon black pepper

2–3 tablespoons minced flat-leaf parsley

- Preheat oven to 400°F.

- Mix Brussels sprouts and carrots. Place on rimmed baking sheet. Drizzle with olive oil and season with salt and pepper. Toss to ensure olive oil coats vegetables.

- Roast for 30 to 40 minutes, stirring once or twice during cooking time.

- Remove vegetables from oven and sprinkle with minced flat-leaf parsley.

SERVES 4 TO 6

GOAT CHEESE SALAD WITH PANCETTA, DRIED CHERRY, AND PORT DRESSING

1¼ cups dried tart cherries

½ cup tawny port

5 ounces pancetta or bacon, chopped

2 shallots, minced

1 clove garlic, minced

⅓ cup olive oil

¼ cup red wine vinegar

2 teaspoons sugar

1 (5.5-ounce) log soft goat cheese, cut into ½-inch slices

1 (5-ounce) bag mixed salad greens

½ cup pine nuts, toasted

- In heavy small saucepan, combine cherries and port. Bring to simmer over medium heat. Remove from heat; allow to stand until cherries swell (approximately 15 minutes).

- In large, heavy skillet, sauté pancetta over medium-low heat until crisp. Add shallots and garlic and cook 2 minutes more. Add oil, vinegar, and sugar. Stir until sugar dissolves.

- Stir cherry mixture into pancetta mixture. Season with salt and pepper. Set skillet aside at room temperature until ready to use.

- Preheat oven to 350°F.

- Place goat cheese slices on rimmed baking sheet and bake until warm (about 10 minutes).

- Combine greens and pine nuts in bowl. Rewarm dressing, pour over salad, and toss. Top with goat cheese and serve.

SERVES 4

PORK WELLINGTON

1 teaspoon fresh rosemary, chopped

½ teaspoon salt

¼ teaspoon pepper

1 sheet frozen puff pastry, thawed

1 (1–1½ pound) pork tenderloin

FILLING

1 tablespoon olive oil

1 small onion, chopped

2 cloves garlic, chopped

1 (6-ounce) bag baby spinach

½ tablespoon salt

¼ teaspoon pepper

2 tablespoons Dijon mustard

- Heat oil in a large skillet over medium heat. Add onion and garlic and cook for 10 minutes.

- Add spinach, ½ tablespoon salt, and ¼ teaspoon pepper. Cook until spinach is wilted and liquid is evaporated. Remove from heat and add mustard. Allow to cool completely.

- Preheat oven to 425°F.

- Mix rosemary, ½ teaspoon salt, and ¼ teaspoon pepper and rub over tenderloin.

- Open thawed pastry sheet on lightly floured surface. Roll out to at least 12 inches in length.

- Spoon cooled onion and spinach mixture into 2-inch-wide mound, down center of pastry.

- Place pork on top of spinach mixture. Wrap pastry over pork, tucking under ends.

- Brush pastry with egg wash (1 egg white plus 1 tablespoon of water).

- Roast for 30 to 35 minutes or until meat thermometer reads 145°F and pastry is golden brown.

- Allow to stand for 10 minutes before serving.

SERVES 4 TO 6

GRENOBLE TART

TART SHELL

⅓ cup unsalted butter

¼ cup granulated sugar

1 egg yolk

1 cup unsifted all-purpose flour

FILLING

2 cups coarsely chopped walnuts

⅔ cup light brown sugar, packed

¼ cup unsalted butter

¼ cup dark corn syrup

½ cup heavy cream

- Preheat oven to 375°F.

- In medium bowl, with wooden spoon or electric mixer, beat butter with sugar until light and fluffy.

- Add egg yolk and beat well.

- Gradually add flour until just blended (mixture should be crumbly).

- With hands, form dough into a ball. Press evenly into bottom and side of 9-inch fluted tart pan with removable bottom. A small overhang can be folded back over to reinforce sides.

- Spread nuts on cookie sheet in single layer and bake at 375°F for 5 minutes. After walnuts cool, sprinkle them in the bottom of art shell.

- In heavy 2-quart saucepan, stir brown sugar with butter, corn syrup, and 2 tablespoons heavy cream. Stirring constantly, bring to boil over medium heat. Boil 1 minute. Pour mixture over walnuts.

- Bake on center rack of 375°F oven for 10 minutes or until mixture is bubbly. Remove from oven and place on a wire rack to cool.

- Beat remaining cream until stiff peaks form. Refrigerate until serving.

- Serve tart at room temperature with whipped cream.

SERVES 6

WINTER

ASHFORD STUD

WINTER FORMAL DINNER

Bacon-Wrapped Water Chestnuts

Blue Cheese Stuffed Cherry Tomatoes

Grilled Romaine Salad with Vinaigrette

Braised Peas and Celery

Veal Bluegrass

Bran Rolls

Grand Marnier Soufflés with Crème Anglaise

John Magnier's Ashford Stud is the American division of his international Coolmore operation based in the horseman's native Ireland. The ambience of Ashford mirrors the old country, with its sturdy stone walls and its wooden barns with high-pitched slate roofs. At the same time, modern touches such as a Polytrack exercise pen for the world-renowned Ashford stallions bespeak the efforts made to provide the best care for the horses. A nursery Magnier established provides Ashford with hundreds of trees to create a park-like setting.

Ashford now occupies more than 1,600 acres, much of which once made up one of Kentucky's most famous cattle farms. Colonel Edmund Taylor, who established Old Taylor Distilleries in Frankfort, introduced imported horned Herefords, which he raised on the farm. During the 1970s Dr. William Lockridge and Robert Hefner IIII converted the farm into a Thoroughbred operation before selling it to a group headed by Magnier.

Coolmore pioneered the practice of standing stallions in both the Northern and Southern hemispheres, taking advantage of the alternating seasons. Among those stallions to have shuttled in recent years are Fusaichi Pegasus, the 2000 Kentucky Derby winner. Another Derby winner, Thunder Gulch, who also won the Belmont Stakes, retired to Ashford after his 1995 Classic year.

Back in Ireland, the Coolmore stallions Sadler's Wells and Danehill were bellwether horses in the years bridging the twentieth and twenty-first centuries. The Magnier group also is a major player in the auction scene, both as purchasers and sellers.

BACON-WRAPPED WATER CHESTNUTS

¾ cup soy sauce

4 tablespoons light brown sugar

24 water chestnuts, drained, rinsed, larger ones halved

12–14 bacon slices, halved

24 wooden toothpicks, soaked in water for 1 hour

- Stir soy sauce and brown sugar together in small bowl.

- Add water chestnuts, stir to coat, and refrigerate, covered, for 1 hour.

- Preheat broiler to 450°F. Remove chestnuts from marinade and discard marinade. Wrap a piece of bacon around each chestnut and secure with wooden toothpick.

- Broil on rack in broiler pan, 2 inches from heat, turning once, until bacon is crisp, 5 to 6 minutes. Serve warm.

MAKES APPROXIMATELY 2 DOZEN

BLUE CHEESE STUFFED CHERRY TOMATOES

1 pint cherry tomatoes (red and yellow if possible)

Salt to taste

⅓ pound good quality blue cheese, mashed

⅔ cup sour cream

1 teaspoon lemon juice

Dash of Tabasco sauce

Paprika and chopped fresh parsley to garnish

- Wash tomatoes, cut off "tops," and scoop out pulp with a melon-ball scooper.

- Lightly sprinkle inside of tomatoes with salt. Drain tomatoes on paper towel, upside down.

- Mix remaining ingredients and stuff tomatoes with mixture.

- Garnish, cover (put in covered container or cover with Saran wrap), and refrigerate. Serve chilled.

MAKES APPROXIMATELY 15 TO 20

GRILLED ROMAINE SALAD WITH VINAIGRETTE

SALAD

18 Roma tomatoes, roasted

¼ cup olive oil

Sea salt, pepper, and garlic powder to taste

4 hearts of romaine lettuce, split lengthwise

2 red onions, thinly sliced

Feta or goat cheese, crumbled

VINAIGRETTE

2 cloves garlic, pressed

4 tablespoons balsamic vinegar

4 tablespoons fresh lemon juice

4 tablespoons creamy Dijon-style mustard

1 tablespoon sea salt

1 tablespoon freshly ground black pepper

½ tablespoon sugar

1½ cups truffle or olive oil

- To roast tomatoes, cut tomatoes in half lengthwise and brush with olive oil. Sprinkle with sea salt, pepper, and garlic powder.

- Place tomatoes, cut side down, in shallow foil-lined pan and bake at 400°F for 30 minutes.

- Wash and drain lettuce; then cut in half lengthwise. Brush cut side with olive oil and season with a little sea salt. Grill, cut side down, on high for 2 minutes.

- Combine vinaigrette ingredients.

- Place romaine lettuce half, grilled side up, on plate and top with roasted tomatoes, sliced onions, and vinaigrette. Sprinkle with cheese.

SERVES 8 TO 10

BRAISED PEAS AND CELERY

2 (10-ounce) packages frozen small
 green peas

2 cups celery, sliced diagonally

1 cup green scallions, sliced

1 cup water

1 teaspoon chicken broth
 or bouillon paste

4 teaspoons cornstarch

2 tablespoons water

2 tablespoons butter

½ teaspoon salt

¼ teaspoon freshly ground
 black pepper

- Mix peas, celery, onions, water, and instant broth in saucepan.
 Bring to boil.

- Reduce heat, cover, and simmer 5 minutes.

- Mix cornstarch with 2 tablespoons water and stir into vegetables.

- Heat, stirring constantly until thickened.

- Stir in butter, salt, and pepper.

SERVES 8 TO 10

VEAL BLUEGRASS

2 tablespoons olive oil

4 mild Italian sausages
 (approximately 4 ounces each)
 cut into 1 inch slices

2 tablespoons butter

1½ pounds boneless veal stew meat
 cut into ½ inch cubes

2 cloves garlic, minced

2 medium onions, chopped

¾ pound mushrooms, cleaned
 and halved

1 red bell pepper, seeded and cubed

1½ cups beef stock

½ cup sherry

1 cup sour cream

2½ tablespoons flour

½ teaspoon salt

Freshly ground black pepper

Freshly ground nutmeg

Chopped fresh flat-leaf parsley

- In large skillet, heat 1 tablespoon of olive oil and partially cook
 sausage until lightly browned. Remove sausage from skillet;
 pour off excess drippings.

- Heat butter and remaining 1 tablespoon olive oil in skillet. Add veal,
 garlic, and onions and brown the veal. Return sausage to skillet and
 cook 2 minutes longer.

- Add mushrooms, red bell pepper, beef stock, and sherry. Bring to
 a slow boil. Reduce heat and simmer partially covered for 1 hour,
 making sure to stir occasionally.

- Dish can be prepared up to this point one day ahead and
 refrigerated.

- Mix sour cream, flour, salt, pepper, and nutmeg. Thoroughly stir
 into veal mixture in the last five minutes while it is simmering.

- Sprinkle with fresh parsley and serve. (This dish goes well with
 rice or noodles. We suggest serving the veal with a wide pasta
 such as fettuccine or with egg noodles.)

SERVES 8 TO 10

BRAN ROLLS

1 cup vegetable shortening

¾ cup sugar

1½ teaspoons salt

1 cup Kellogg's All-Bran cereal

1 cup boiling water

2 eggs, beaten

2 packages dry yeast

1 cup lukewarm water

6 cups flour, sifted

Butter, melted (for brushing
  the tops)

3 7x11-inch pans

- Combine shortening, sugar, salt, and bran cereal in large mixing bowl.

- Pour in boiling water and stir until shortening is dissolved. Let cool until lukewarm; then mix in eggs.

- Sprinkle yeast on lukewarm water in glass measuring cup. Stir with fork to moisten yeast and let sit 1 to 2 minutes. Stir again until yeast is completely dissolved. Stir into cereal mixture.

- Add flour 1 cup at a time, using a whisk or spoon for the first 4 cups. Use hands to mix in last 2 cups. Let dough rise in warm place (in front of open door of 225°F oven), covered with a warm, wet towel for 1 hour.

- Cover bowl with plastic wrap and refrigerate dough 8 hours or overnight.

- Punch down dough in bowl with fist to let air escape. Remove dough from bowl and divide in half. Roll out dough, half batch at a time, on lightly floured surface to ¼-inch thickness. The "scraps" of dough from both batches can be combined and rolled out a second time. Roll out a little thinner because it will draw up.

- Cut out rolls with a 2½-inch biscuit cutter and lift from board with a narrow, metal spatula, lightly coated with flour. Dip half of the circle in melted butter, fold in half, and gently press edges together. Place in shallow pan, buttered half down, with sides nearly touching. Brush tops with butter, cover pan with wax paper, and allow rolls to rise for 2 hours.

- Bake at 400°F for 10 to 12 minutes until browned.
  (Note: These rolls freeze well.)

MAKES APPROXIMATELY 4 DOZEN ROLLS

INDIVIDUAL GRAND MARNIER SOUFFLÉS WITH CRÈME ANGLAISE

2 tablespoons butter, softened

8 teaspoons sugar

6 egg yolks (large eggs)

½ cup sugar

¼ cup Grand Marnier liqueur

1½ teaspoons pure vanilla extract

Grated zest of 1 large orange

8 egg whites (large eggs)

¼ teaspoon cream of tartar

⅛ teaspoon salt

- Preheat oven to 375°F. Grease 8 (8-ounce) ramekins (or 2-quart soufflé dish) with butter and sprinkle each dish with 1 teaspoon sugar, turning to coat.

- Place egg yolks in large bowl and beat with electric mixer at medium-high speed 2 to 3 minutes or until thick and pale.

- Gradually add ½ cup sugar and beat until blended.

- Beat in liqueur, vanilla, and orange zest.

- Place egg whites in clean large bowl and beat at high speed one minute or until foamy. Add cream of tartar and salt. Beat until soft peaks form.

- Place a heavy baking sheet on middle oven rack to warm.

- Gently stir ¼ of egg whites into liqueur mixture.

- Gently fold in the remaining egg whites and divide evenly among prepared ramekins or fill single soufflé dish.

- Place ramekins or soufflé dish on baking sheet in oven. Bake at 375°F for 15 minutes or until golden brown.

- Serve immediately with Grand Marnier Crème Anglaise.

SERVES 8 TO 10

GRAND MARNIER CRÈME ANGLAISE

6 egg yolks (extra-large eggs)

⅔ cups sugar

1½ cups hot whole milk

1 tablespoon pure vanilla extract

2 tablespoons Grand Marnier liqueur

- Whisk egg yolks in 2-quart saucepan, adding sugar by large spoonfuls. Beat 2 to 3 minutes until yolks turn pale yellow and thick.

- With wooden spoon, slowly stir in hot milk. Do not beat.

- Set saucepan over moderately low heat and stir slowly all over bottom of pan. Do not bring to simmer, but heat enough to thicken sauce. The sauce is done when it coats the spoon and when drawing your finger across the coated spoon leaves a line.

- Remove from heat and whisk in vanilla and Grand Marnier. Serve warm. (Note: Sauce may be made a day ahead and kept refrigerated until ready to use.)

MAKES ABOUT 2 CUPS

CRESTWOOD FARM

WINTER BUFFET

Herbed Tomatoes

Fruit Salad with Vinaigrette Dressing

Sour Cream Biscuits

Buttered Kentucky Asparagus

Chicken Tetrazzini

Lemon Curd Tarts

Pope McLean had planned to follow his father into medicine when Thoroughbreds took hold of his heart, sending him in a new direction. Young Pope McLean became hooked after raising Oil Wick, winner of the 1959 Kentucky Jockey Club Stakes, on behalf of his father and P.A.B. Widener II. Upon graduation from the University of Kentucky, McLean entered a two-year apprenticeship at Calumet Farm. Shortly thereafter, a few broodmare acquisitions started McLean on his own path, and he leased a farm and began boarding mares and breeding and selling yearlings.

By 1970 his operation was ready for more growth, and he leased nearly five hundred acres. Within a couple of years, McLean was able to purchase the farm, where the boarding operation continues to flourish. McLean's operation has produced more than 180 stakes horses for himself and for clients, including Xtra Heat, Island Fashion, and Serena's Song, each of whom was foaled and raised at Crestwood, and each of whom earned more than $2 million.

In the early 1990s McLean's sons Pope Jr. and Marc, followed by daughter Grandison, completed college and rejoined the operation they had grown up working in. Together the McLeans expanded Crestwood's focus in 1994 to include a stallion division. Success came quickly to the stallion roster, with Storm Boot emerging as the first successful son of Storm Cat, siring more than fifty stakes winners. Petionville sired Alabama Stakes winner Island Fashion among some twenty stakes winners, and Dixieland Heat's daughter, Xtra Heat, was the champion three-year-old filly of 2001. Although the operation has now grown to encompass more than 1,000 acres, the headquarters remains to this day at the original Spurr Road site.

HERBED TOMATOES

1 pint cherry tomatoes or grape tomatoes

Garlic salt

Parmigiano Reggiano cheese

Assorted fresh herbs

- Rinse tomatoes in colander. Do not dry.

- Place in large resealable plastic bag and sprinkle with garlic salt.

- Grate Parmigiano Reggiano over tomatoes.

- In food processor, chop assortment of fresh herbs such as basil, thyme, oregano, dill, flat-leaf parsley.

- Put chopped herbs in with tomatoes, season with salt and pepper. Seal bag, shake well, and pour into serving bowl.

SERVES 8 TO 10

SOUR CREAM BISCUITS

2 cups self-rising flour, unsifted

2 sticks unsalted butter, melted

1 (8-ounce) carton sour cream

- Mix flour, butter, and sour cream and put into small muffin tins.

- Bake in preheated 400°F oven for 20 minutes or bake in preheated 450°F oven for 10 to 12 minutes.

- These freeze well. They are also good with honey, jam, or jelly for breakfast.

MAKES 24

CHICKEN TETRAZZINI

4 cups cooked chicken breasts

16 ounces (1 pound) fresh sliced mushrooms

4 tablespoons butter

2 small onions, diced

4 tablespoons flour

1½ cups rich chicken stock

2 pints heavy cream

¾ teaspoon and ½ tablespoon salt

Paprika to taste

¼ teaspoon cayenne pepper

1 (8-ounce) box spaghetti

2 cups mild cheddar cheese, grated

Cheddar cheese for garnish

- Cut chicken into bite-sized pieces.

- Sauté sliced mushrooms in 2 tablespoons butter and drain liquid. Remove mushrooms from pan and set aside. Sauté diced onions in 2 tablespoons butter until soft.

- In large heavy pan, mix 4 tablespoons flour with cooled chicken. Combine chicken, chicken stock, cream, and sautéed onions and mushrooms. Season with ¾ teaspoon salt, paprika, and ¼ teaspoon cayenne pepper. Heat, stirring constantly, until hot. Cook a second or two after mixture has bubbled.

- In large pot, add ½ tablespoon salt to water and bring to boil. Add spaghetti. Undercook by 1½ minutes. Drain well.

- Mix spaghetti and cheese with chicken mixture. Put into a greased 9x13-inch casserole dish. Bake in preheated 325°F oven for 30 to 40 minutes, until casserole is bubbling. Sprinkle with more cheese, allow to melt slightly, and serve.

SERVES 8 TO 10

BUTTERED KENTUCKY ASPARAGUS

2 pounds asparagus

⅓ cup melted unsalted butter

1 tablespoon lemon juice

- Wash and trim asparagus to equal length.

- Cook in boiling water in a saucepan 5 to 8 minutes or until crisp-tender. Drain and plunge into ice water to stop cooking process. Drain again.

- Top with melted butter and lemon juice.

SERVES 8

FRUIT SALAD WITH VINAIGRETTE DRESSING

SALAD

8 cups baby spinach

1½ cups grapefruit segments

1½ cups fresh sliced strawberries

1 cup fresh blackberries

1 large avocado, sliced

1½ cups fresh peaches, sliced

Mint leaves for garnish

VINAIGRETTE DRESSING

1 (10-ounce) jar seedless blackberry preserves

½ cup red wine vinegar

1 large clove garlic, minced

1 teaspoon salt

1 teaspoon lemon pepper

1½ cups vegetable oil

- Gently combine spinach, grapefruit segments, sliced strawberries, blackberries, avocado, and peaches.

- For dressing, put preserves, vinegar, garlic, salt, and lemon pepper in a food processor. Pulse until blended. With processor running, pour vegetable oil through chute in a slow stream and blend until smooth.

- Garnish fruit salad with mint leaves and serve with the vinaigrette dressing on the side.

DRESSING MAKES 2 CUPS; SERVES 8 TO 10

LEMON CURD TARTS

PASTRY

2 cups flour

½ teaspoon salt

½ cup cold, unsalted butter

5 tablespoons cold water

FILLING

½ cup unsalted butter

½ cup fresh lemon juice (3–4 lemons)

3 teaspoons freshly grated lemon zest (4 lemons)

1½ cups sugar

5 eggs, beaten

- Preheat oven to 425°F.

- Combine flour and salt in a bowl. Cut in butter with a pastry blender until pieces are the size of small peas. Sprinkle water gradually over flour mixture, stirring with a fork and drawing flour into a ball. Add just enough water to hold the mixture together and pull away from the sides of the bowl.

- Pat dough into a ball and turn out onto lightly floured surface. Roll out into circle and cut shapes to fit small muffin tins. Prick each shell with fork. Bake for 12 minutes. Cool.

- For filling, melt butter in saucepan. Add lemon juice, zest, and sugar. Cook, stirring until sugar is dissolved.

- Add eggs and cook, stirring constantly, until thick, about 5 to 10 minutes.

- To avoid lumps, scrape filling into a medium-mesh sieve. Set over bowl and strain. Allow to cool slightly before filling pastry shells.

MAKES APPROXIMATELY 20

GAINESWAY FARM

WINTER COCKTAILS

Hummus

White Corn Bisque

Filet de Boeuf à la Crème Tomate

Crustless Spinach Tart

Mahogany Glazed Salmon

Bourbon Truffles

Oatmeal Lace Cookies

Gainesway Farm embodies many decades of American racing tradition combined with the growing international flavor of the Turf. In 1989 Graham Beck, a leading mining executive, vintner, and sportsman in South Africa, purchased the storied farm, the first in the Thoroughbred world to gain accredited arboretum status, from John R. Gaines. Beck's son, Antony, and Antony's wife, Angela Levy Beck, live on the 1,500-acre farm, where the requirements of pasture management and equine husbandry co-exist with horticultural planning and design.

The property once had been part of the Whitney family estates established by Harry Payne Whitney early in the twentieth century and later maintained in separate parcels by C.V. Whitney and John Hay Whitney. Kentucky Derby winner Regret and other champions such as Equipoise and Top Flight grace the farm's history from the Whitney era.

Gaines established an internationally renowned stallion operation at Gainesway in the 1970s and early '80s, standing such leading sires as Vaguely Noble, Blushing Groom, Lyphard, and Riverman and creating an award-winning compound of artistic buildings with graceful arches and sculpted metal doors. His philosophy was to treat his stallions "like kings." Incorporating the unique beauties of Gainesway with a strong business ethic, Antony Beck and his father have continued the traditions. Contemporary stars of the stallion barns include champion Afleet Alex, winner of the Preakness and Belmont stakes in 2005, as well as veteran leading sire Cozzene. Appropriately, Birdstone, winner of the 2004 Belmont Stakes for C.V.'s widow, Marylou Whitney, also stands there, linking past with present.

HUMMUS

2 cups canned chickpeas, drained (reserve liquid)

3 garlic cloves, minced

1 teaspoon salt

⅓ cup tahini (sesame paste)

Juice from 2 lemons

2 tablespoons reserved chickpea liquid

1 tablespoon crushed red pepper flakes

- Place all ingredients in food processor and process until smooth.

- Refrigerate or serve at room temperature with crackers or cut raw vegetables.

MAKES 2 CUPS

WHITE CORN BISQUE

2 tablespoons olive oil

5 stalks celery, diced

4 cloves garlic, peeled and roughly chopped

2 sprigs fresh thyme

4 cups fresh white corn kernels

Salt and freshly ground black pepper to taste

10 cups chicken stock

2 cups heavy cream

Grilled French bread croutons

- Place oil in saucepot over medium heat. Add celery, garlic, and thyme. Cook until ingredients are soft, about 2 to 4 minutes. Do not brown.

- Add corn, salt, and pepper. Cook for 2 minutes.

- Add chicken stock and simmer for 15 minutes. Add heavy cream. Lower heat and cook gently for 5 minutes. Remove pot from heat.

- Discard thyme. Pour half of the soup into mixing bowl and purée with an immersion blender or regular blender.

- Pour purée back into pot and adjust seasoning with additional salt and pepper.

- Serve with grilled croutons.

SERVES 10 TO 12

FILET DE BOEUF À LA CRÈME TOMATE

¼ pound (1 stick) butter, softened

1 whole tenderloin

- Preheat oven to 500 degrees.

- Spread butter all over meat, put in roasting pan, and place in hot oven.

- Immediately reduce heat to 350 degrees; bake for 20 minutes or until meat thermometer registers 120 degrees.

- Allow meat to cool; then refrigerate.

- When ready to use, cut meat into thin slices and spread each slice with crème tomate.

- Roll meat slices up lengthwise and arrange on tray.

CRÈME TOMATE

¼ cup minced onions

2 tablespoons butter

4 large ripe tomatoes, peeled, seeded, and chopped, or 4 canned tomatoes, drained

½ teaspoon salt

¼ teaspoon cracked pepper

¼ teaspoon sugar

Pinch of thyme

1 bay leaf

1 (8 ounce) package cream cheese

2 cloves garlic, peeled and crushed

2 tablespoons basil

⅛ teaspoon Tabasco sauce

½ cup heavy cream

- Saute onions in butter until soft; add tomatoes, salt, pepper, sugar Thyme, and bay leaf.

- Simmer, covered, over low heat for 10 to 12 minutes.

- Remove cover and cook over medium-high heat for 10 minutes or until much of the liquid has evaporated and the sauce is very thick.

- Strain through a sieve and cool.

- Place ¾ cup sauce in the container of a blender or food processor.

- Add remaining ingredients and blend for 5 to 6 seconds.

- Chill until ready to use.

CRUSTLESS SPINACH TART

2 (8-ounce) packages frozen
    leaf spinach

2 pounds fresh ricotta cheese

5 eggs

3 tablespoons fresh dill, chopped

1 teaspoon salt

1 teaspoon black pepper

6–8 ounces cherry tomatoes

6–8 ounces feta cheese, crumbled

- Preheat oven to 320°F.

- Defrost spinach and squeeze water completely out.

- Mix spinach with ricotta cheese, eggs, dill, salt, and pepper.

- Pour mixture into 9x12-inch casserole dish.

- Cut tomatoes in half and place cut side up on top of spinach mixture. Sprinkle with feta cheese.

- Bake at 320°F until pie is set, approximately 1 hour. Cut into squares and serve.

SERVES 10 TO 12

MAHOGANY GLAZED SALMON

2 cups sugar

⅔ cup of water

10 cloves garlic, peeled and crushed

3–4 ounces fresh ginger, sliced
    with skin on

1 cup soy sauce

- Mix sugar and water in heavy saucepan and bring to a simmer over medium-low heat. Be sure sugar dissolves completely. Swirl pan (*do not stir*) as you bring mixture to a boil. Cover saucepan with tight lid for about 10 minutes, allowing any sugar crystals to dissolve. Uncover saucepan and swirl again and liquid will start to color.

- When liquid is golden brown, add garlic and ginger. Continue to boil until syrup is a dark golden brown. Add soy sauce carefully, stir, and cook a few more minutes. Glaze should be very dark brown by now.

- Cool slightly, strain, and brush over salmon at least 2 to 3 times over an 8-hour period.

- Bake salmon at 450°F for 12 minutes per inch of thickness.

- Serve with whole-wheat party squares or other wheat crackers.

MAKES ENOUGH GLAZE FOR 1 LARGE FILET OF SALMON

BOURBON TRUFFLES

8 ounces semisweet chocolate, chopped

½ cup (1 stick) unsalted butter

⅔ cup finely crushed gingersnap cookies

3 tablespoons of quality bourbon

½ cup chopped pecans

½ cup unsweetened cocoa powder

½ cup powdered (confectioner's) sugar

- Melt chocolate and butter in heavy saucepan over low heat, stirring continuously.

- Add crushed gingersnaps, bourbon, and nuts. Pour into bowl and cover to chill at least 1 hour or until firm.

- Taking a pinch (approximately 1½ teaspoons) of dough, roll each by hand into round balls.

- Sift cocoa powder and powdered sugar in shallow bowl. Roll each rounded truffle in cocoa/sugar mixture.

- Allow truffles to stand 10 minutes at room temperature before serving.

YIELDS APPROXIMATELY 24 TRUFFLES

OATMEAL LACE COOKIES

2½ cups regular oats

1 cup brown sugar, packed

2 teaspoons baking powder

½ cup (1 stick) unsalted butter, melted

1 egg, beaten

- Preheat oven to 350°F.

- Combine oats, brown sugar, and baking powder; pour in melted butter and mix thoroughly. Beat in egg.

- Drop by teaspoonfuls onto parchment paper-lined or greased cookie sheet. Make sure to allow room between cookies as they will spread as they cook.

- Bake at 350°F for 8 to 10 minutes or just until edges start to brown.

- Allow cookies to cool 1 to 2 minutes before removing from cookie sheet.

MAKES APPROXIMATELY 24 COOKIES

MILL RIDGE FARM

CHRISTMAS FOR TWELVE

Pâté with Toast Points

Mushroom Bisque

Three Pear Salad with Spicy Pecans

Broccoli with Roasted Red Peppers

Mill Ridge Scalloped Potatoes

Standing Prime Rib Roast and Horseradish Sauce

Icebox Rolls

Kentucky Bourbon Cake and Egg Nog

Alice Chandler and her family are integral to the history of the Bluegrass. Her grandfather bred and owned Thoroughbreds, and her father, Hal Price Headley, left his own unique footprints. As a prime force behind Keeneland, with its seventy-plus years of racing tradition and its international sales arm, Headley provided a lasting influence on the horse industry and sport.

Headley owned some four thousand acres of farmland, under the names of Beaumont and La Belle farms. The last parcel of land he bought was the 286 acres he left to one of his daughters, Alice. She named the property Mill Ridge and has added property so that the farm now covers more than a thousand acres. True to her heritage in the hands-on husbandry of horse agriculture as well as involvement in the running of the sport, Chandler has served many roles — breeder, owner, trainer — all the while raising and prepping horses for an international clientele. She also has served numerous organizations, including the Kentucky Thoroughbred Association as president.

Chandler bred and sold Sir Ivor, who in 1968 won the Epsom Derby to create a breakthrough for American-breds at the top levels of European racing. Prominent horses she has raised for clients include champions Point Given and Sweet Catomine and 2005 Kentucky Derby winner Giacomo.

Mill Ridge also maintains a prime stallion roster, which has included Gone West and Diesis. Chandler is assisted by three sons, Headley, Reynolds, and Mike Bell, while her husband, Dr. John Chandler, is president of the American division of Prince Khalid Abdullah's Juddmonte Farms.

PÂTÉ WITH TOAST POINTS

1 pound chicken livers,
  fresh or frozen

1 small onion, peeled and sliced

¾ cup chicken stock

¾ cup unsalted butter, softened

1 tablespoon brandy, cognac,
  or sherry

1 tablespoon Worcestershire sauce

¼ teaspoon nutmeg

½ teaspoon paprika

½ teaspoon curry powder

⅛ teaspoon ground cloves

1 teaspoon salt

¼ teaspoon black pepper

- Simmer livers and onions in chicken broth for 10 minutes turning them once. Drain well.

- In a blender or food processor, purée the warm (not hot) livers with butter, brandy, Worcestershire sauce, and seasonings.

- Pack in small greased mold or bowl. Chill.

- Unmold and serve cold with toast points.

SERVES 12

MUSHROOM BISQUE

1 cup (2 sticks) unsalted butter

6 cups mushrooms, sliced

8 tablespoons flour

½ teaspoon dry mustard

2 teaspoons salt

5 cups chicken broth

1 bay leaf

4 cups half & half

½ cup chives, chopped

½ cup sherry

Sour cream and flat-leaf parsley
  to garnish

- Melt butter in large saucepan over medium heat. Add mushrooms and sauté until tender.

- Add flour, mustard, and salt, stirring constantly for approximately 1 minute. Flour should not brown.

- Add broth and bay leaf and cook uncovered at low temperature until mixture thickens.

- Slowly stir in half & half and add chives. Heat thoroughly but do not boil. Remove bay leaf and add sherry just before serving.

- Garnish with sour cream and top with sprig of flat-leaf parsley.

SERVES 12

BROCCOLI WITH ROASTED RED PEPPERS

10 cups broccoli florets

2 tablespoons butter

2 cloves garlic, minced

½ cup diced roasted red peppers

¼ teaspoon black pepper

1 teaspoon salt

1 tablespoon lemon juice

- Steam broccoli for 5 to 8 minutes or until crisp-tender.

- Sauté garlic in butter, stir in red peppers, and add salt and pepper and lemon juice. Transfer broccoli to a large bowl; add red pepper mixture and toss to coat.

SERVES 12

THREE PEAR SALAD WITH SPICY PECANS

3 heads of Boston lettuce, cleaned and dried

6 pears, 2 each of Anjou, Bosc, and Bartlett, unpeeled and sliced thin

Stilton cheese, crumbled for garnish

Pomegranate seeds for garnish

SPICY PECANS

3 tablespoons butter

¼ teaspoon garlic powder

3 tablespoons Worcestershire sauce

¼ teaspoon cayenne pepper

1 teaspoon salt, more to salt after baked

Dash of Tabasco sauce

½ teaspoon ground cinnamon

1 pound pecan halves

VINAIGRETTE:

1 tablespoon pomegranate molasses

1 tablespoon balsamic vinegar

1 teaspoon Dijon mustard

3 tablespoons olive oil

3 tablespoons canola oil

Pinch of salt

Freshly ground black pepper

- Preheat oven to 300°F.

- In heavy skillet heat butter until melted. Add all ingredients but pecans. Stir until blended, add pecans, and toss until coated.

- Place on a cookie sheet in a single layer and toast for 15–20 minutes, stirring once or twice.

- Remove from oven; salt generously. Cool on paper towel and store in air-tight container. Will keep for weeks!

- Mix molasses, vinegar, and mustard. Slowly add olive oil and canola oil. Season with salt and pepper.

- Toss lettuce with pears, cheese, pomegranate seeds, and spicy pecans. Drizzle with vinaigrette and serve.

SERVES 12

MILL RIDGE SCALLOPED POTATOES

3 pounds (about 8 cups) Yukon Gold or russet potatoes, peeled

3 cups milk

2½ cups heavy cream

1 large or 2 small cloves garlic, peeled, crushed, and minced to purée

1 teaspoon salt

¾ cup teaspoon freshly ground white pepper

1½ tablespoons butter

1½ cups grated Swiss cheese

1¼ cups grated Parmesan cheese to sprinkle on top

- Preheat oven to 400°F.

- Rinse potatoes well and dry thoroughly. Slice potatoes ⅛-inch thick into large saucepan. Add milk, cream, garlic, salt, and pepper and bring liquid to boil over moderate heat, stirring with wooden spatula to prevent scorching. Remove pan from heat.

- Pour potato mixture into well-buttered gratin dish or shallow baking dish.

- Sprinkle grated Swiss and Parmesan cheese over mixture and place dish on baking sheet. Bake at 400°F for about 1 hour. Potatoes are done when nicely browned and tip of knife pierces potato easily.

- Let dish stand for 15 to 20 minutes before serving.

SERVES 12

STANDING PRIME RIB ROAST

10-pound rib roast

2 tablespoons fresh cooking oil

Freshly ground black pepper

Optional rosemary, thyme, or garlic

Salt

- Remove roast from refrigerator 2 to 3 hours before cooking.

- Preheat oven to 450°F.

- Place roast on rack in shallow pan and rub with oil, freshly ground black pepper, and, if desired, a little rosemary, thyme, garlic, or all three. Salt just before putting in oven.

- Roast 30 minutes. Reduce heat to 325°F and continue to roast, allowing about 12 minutes per pound for rare (meat thermometer 120–125°F) or 14 to 15 minutes per pound for medium (thermometer 140°F).

- Allow to stand 10 minutes before carving.

- Serve with horseradish sauce (recipe below).

SERVES 12

HORSERADISH SAUCE

½ pound horseradish root, peeled

1 cup fresh bread crumbs

2–3 tablespoons milk

2 tablespoons sugar

1 teaspoon dry mustard

2 tablespoons vinegar

Salt and pepper to taste

1 cup heavy cream

- Grate or finely grind peeled fresh horseradish root in food processor.

- Add fresh bread crumbs moistened with a few tablespoons of milk, plus sugar, dry mustard diluted with vinegar, and pinch of salt.

- Fold in heavy cream, lightly whipped. Season sauce with salt and pepper to taste and chill.

ICE BOX ROLLS

½ cup vegetable shortening

6 tablespoons sugar

½ cup boiling water

1 package dry yeast, dissolved in ½ cup warm water

1 egg, beaten

½ teaspoon salt

3–3¼ cups flour

1 stick of unsalted butter for dipping

- Cream shortening and sugar; add boiling water. Cool to lukewarm and add yeast, egg, and salt.

- Stir in enough flour to make soft dough. Cover and place in refrigerator overnight or until needed.

- Make rolls in desired shape; dip in melted butter. Place in 2 9x9-inch baking pans and let rise 1 to 2 hours. Bake at 400°F for 15 minutes. (Note: 1 cake of yeast dissolved in ½ cup cold water may be substituted for dry yeast mixture.)

MAKES 1½ DOZEN

KENTUCKY BOURBON CAKE

1 pound candied red cherries
 (cut in half)

½ pound golden raisins

1 pint (2 cups) Kentucky bourbon,
 plus ¾ cup extra

¾ pound unsalted butter

2 cups sugar

1 cup brown sugar

6 eggs, separated

5 cups flour (sift before measuring)

2 teaspoons nutmeg

1 teaspoon baking powder

1 pound pecans, halved

- Soak the cherries and raisins in 2 cups of bourbon overnight or longer.

- Cream butter and sugars until fluffy. Add egg yolks one at a time and beat mixture well.

- Add soaked fruit and bourbon; then add flour, reserving some flour for the pecans.

- Add nutmeg and baking powder. Fold in beaten egg whites. Lastly add pecans that have been lightly tossed in remaining flour.

- Pour batter in large greased tube pan (angel food cake pan) lined with greased wax paper or parchment paper. Place tube pan on large shallow pan of hot water in oven for baking. Bake in slow oven (250–275°F) for 3 to 4 hours. Test with broom straw or toothpick to be sure cake is cooked through. Toothpick or straw should come out clean when cake is done.

- After cake is cooled, slowly pour remaining ¾ cup of bourbon over cake. Wrap tightly in plastic wrap and store in refrigerator for several weeks.

SERVES 12

EGG NOG

12 eggs, separated

2 cups powdered sugar

1 pint (2 cups) good bourbon

1 teaspoon nutmeg, finely grated

3 pints (6 cups) whipping cream,
 beaten until stiff

- Beat egg yolks and add sugar and nutmeg. Add bourbon slowly. This will cook eggs.

- Fold in beaten egg whites. Fold in whipped cream.

- The eggnog will have a thick consistency and is often served in silver julep cups with a spoon.

SERVES 12

PAYSON STUD

WINTER BUFFET

Parmesan Cups with Goat Cheese Filling

Mixed Greens with Green Goddess Dressing

Sautéed Spinach

Roasted Carrots with Shallots and Balsamic Vinegar

Crown Roast of Pork with Apple Stuffing

Bananas Foster

Charles and Virginia Kraft Payson established Payson Stud in 1980 on property that had been portions of Greentree Stud and the T.A. Grissom Farm. The Paysons soon began turning out major winners, including 1984 Travers Stakes winner Carr de Naskra. Mrs. Payson continued the operation after the 1985 death of her husband and campaigned the international champion St. Jovite. After St. Jovite won the King George VI and Queen Elizabeth Stakes at Ascot, Mrs. Payson was presented the trophy by Queen Elizabeth.

In 2002 Mrs. Payson had the unique accomplishment of being the breeder of two Eclipse Award winners — Vindication and Farda Amiga. Additionally, Mrs. Payson's Northern Sunset was named Broodmare of the Year for 1995.

As home to outstanding Thoroughbreds, Payson Stud includes structures of unique historical context. In the late 1700s, what is believed to be the oldest brick building in the area served as both a temporary home while the manor house was under construction and a stopover for travelers between Paris and Lexington. Combining the requirements of hospitality with pragmatic protection of his family, the owner placed overnight guests in an upstairs room accessible only by outside ladder, which was removed once they were safely ensconced for the night. Today this building is Mrs. Payson's office, to which access and egress are less arduous.

The manor house burned to the ground twice between 1801 and 1850. Renowned architect James McMurtry is responsible for its present design. Regarded as one of the purest examples of the neoclassical style of the mid-nineteenth century, its Greek Revival facade features a portico supported by four Corinthian columns.

PARMESAN CUPS WITH GOAT CHEESE FILLING

PARMESAN CUPS

3 cups Parmesan cheese, finely
   grated

GOAT CHEESE FILLING

18 ounces goat cheese

6 tablespoons fresh basil, diced

½ to ¾ cup heavy cream

Kosher salt to taste

Black pepper to taste

Paprika for garnish

- Preheat oven to 375°F and line baking sheet with parchment paper.

- Sprinkle 2 tablespoons of finely grated Parmesan cheese into 2-inch circles on parchment paper, allowing space between each circle. (They will spread as they cook.)

- Bake 6 to 7 minutes. Remove from oven and allow to cool only a few seconds.

- Working quickly, invert the Parmesan circles over prepared basket form (We suggest an inverted muffin tin or some aluminum foil covering the bottom of a glass.) Gently press the cheese into basket form.

- Allow to cool completely before removing.

- These can be made a day ahead and stored in plastic resealable bags.

- Mix the filling ingredients well.

- Pipe or spoon mixture into individual Parmesan cups.

- Sprinkle with paprika and serve.

SERVES 12 TO 18

MIXED GREENS WITH GREEN GODDESS DRESSING

3 large bags of mixed greens,
   cleaned and patted dry

GREEN GODDESS DRESSING

1 cup mayonnaise

½ cup sour cream

1 clove garlic, minced

⅓ cup flat-leaf parsley, minced

3 tablespoons scallions, minced

½ teaspoon each, salt and pepper

2 tablespoons tarragon vinegar

1 tablespoon lemon juice

1 tablespoon anchovy paste

- Combine all dressing ingredients in food processor or blender. Refrigerate overnight.

- Serve over mixed greens salad.

SERVES 12

SAUTÉED SPINACH

6 tablespoons butter

6 tablespoons sesame oil

3 cloves garlic, minced

6 tablespoons fresh ginger root, grated

3–4 (6-ounce) bags fresh spinach

3 tablespoons brown sugar

3 tablespoons sherry

6 tablespoons soy sauce

- In large skillet, sauté garlic and ginger in butter and sesame oil for 2 minutes. Add spinach and toss until wilted.

- Remove from heat.

- Dissolve brown sugar in sherry and soy sauce. Pour mixture over spinach and serve at once.

SERVES 12

ROASTED CARROTS WITH SHALLOTS AND BALSAMIC VINEGAR

2 pounds of carrots, cleaned and sliced on the diagonal into wedges

5 shallots, minced

2–3 tablespoons olive oil

Salt and pepper to taste

2 tablespoons balsamic vinegar

- Preheat oven to 425°F.

- Place first 4 ingredients in baking pan, tossing to ensure oil covers carrots.

- Roast in oven for approximately 20 to 25 minutes until slightly browned, stirring once during cooking.

- Remove from oven and drizzle with balsamic vinegar.

- Serve immediately.

SERVES 12

CROWN ROAST OF PORK

2 pork loin rib roasts (This equals about 24 ribs or 14 pounds total) (Note: A butcher can trim and remove the membrane between each rib and shape roasts into a "crown.")

2 teaspoons each: black, green, and white peppercorns

3 large cloves garlic, diced

2 tablespoons sea salt

Olive oil

Whole herbs for garnish (rosemary, sage, thyme, etc.)

- Bring pork roasts to room temperature and tie roasts together with kitchen twine in a circle or "crown." Place in roasting pan with bone ends up and bone tips covered with foil to prevent burning.

- Preheat oven to 250°F.

- Grind peppercorns in spice grinder. Mix ground pepper with garlic, salt, and enough olive oil to allow for brushing on the pork.

- Brush entire surface of roast with spice and oil mixture.

- Insert digital meat thermometer.

- Roast meat to an internal temperature of 130°F; then increase oven temperature to 350°F and continue cooking until meat's internal temperature reaches 145°F. (This takes about 1½ hours to get to 130°F and about 10 minutes to reach 145°F internally.)

- Remove roast from oven and allow to rest for about 10 minutes.

- Place roast on serving platter; remove twine and foil.

- Fill center of "crown" with cooked apple stuffing, if desired.

- Garnish platter with herbs. (Note: An internal temperature of 145°F will increase by 3 to 4 degrees during the resting period. This brings roast to point where it has lost the last of its pink color and is still very juicy. A roast cooked to 160°F internally is too dry for our liking.)

SERVES 12 TO 14

APPLE STUFFING

1 cup raisins, dried cherries,
  or dried cranberries

3 sticks (¾ pound) butter

1½ large onions, chopped

8–10 stalks celery, chopped

4 tart apples, peeled, cored,
  and diced

3 teaspoons each: ground
  coriander, marjoram, nutmeg,
  and black pepper

2 teaspoons salt

2 (16-ounce) packages Pepperidge
  Farm Cornbread Stuffing

1½ cups chopped almonds
  (optional)

1–1½ cups chicken broth

- Steep raisins, cherries, or cranberries in boiling water until plump. Drain.

- Melt butter in large skillet. Add chopped onion, celery, and apples. Sauté for 5 minutes.

- In a large bowl, add ground spices and salt to dry stuffing mix.

- Combine onion mixture, stuffing, raisins (and/or cranberries or cherries). Add nuts at this time if using.

- Add chicken broth and mix well until mixture achieves moist consistency.

- Form stuffing into balls or place in casserole dish.

- Bake at 350°F, 30 to 40 minutes covered. (Note: This dish may be prepared 1 day ahead and then baked.)

SERVES 12 TO 14

BANANAS FOSTER

12 tablespoons (1½ sticks)
  unsalted butter

1½ cups dark brown sugar

2 teaspoons cinnamon

6 bananas, halved lengthwise
  and each side cut in half

2 ounces banana liqueur

1 cup dark rum, warmed

1 quart vanilla ice cream

¼ cup chopped pecans (optional)

- In large, heavy frying pan, melt butter over low heat.

- Blend in sugar and cinnamon. Stir until sugar is dissolved.

- Add bananas and liqueur. Baste bananas with sauce and cook 1 minute, stirring gently.

- Carefully pour warmed rum over bananas and sauce. Ignite rum and baste fruit until flames burn out.

- Serve over vanilla ice cream. Garnish with chopped pecans.

SERVES 12 TO 14

SHADWELL FARM

WINTER CASUAL SUPPER

Winner's Circle Cheese Mold

Sour Cream Cornbread

Winter Greens

Marinated Cole Slaw

Crisp Parmesan Potatoes

Shadwell's Venison Marinade

Oatmeal Cake with Coconut Pecan Topping

One of the divisions of the vast Thoroughbred holdings of the Maktoum family, the rulers of Dubai, is the international group of farms owned by Sheikh Hamdan al Maktoum. The older brother of ruler Sheikh Mohammed, Sheikh Hamdan is Dubai's minister of finance and operates Shadwell properties in Kentucky and England. Shadwell Farm in Kentucky, under direction of vice president and general manager Rick Nichols, has grown from the original 700 acres to 3,400 acres. The immaculate fields are dotted with handsome, blue-trimmed gray barns, and plaques reminiscent of medallions are featured on gateway pillars throughout the complex.

Both a breeder and buyer of bloodstock, Sheikh Hamdan is a major investor at Keeneland yearling sales. Looking further afield, Sheikh Hamdan also bought Invasor, who was bred in Argentina and was hailed as a champion while racing in Uruguay. For his new owner, Invasor won the Breeders' Cup Classic and other races in this country in 2006 and was voted Horse of the Year. The following year he won the Dubai World Cup, naturally a cherished event to his owner.

Nashwan, who was foaled at Shadwell, won the Epsom Derby in England for Sheikh Hamdan in 1989. Nashwan was foaled from Height of Fashion, a mare purchased from Queen Elizabeth II. He is commemorated by the name Nashwan Stud, affixed to Shadwell's Kentucky stallion division. Only five years after Nashwan's victory, Shadwell homebred Erhaab also won the historic Epsom Derby. Another outstanding Shadwell-bred, Sakhee won the 2001 Prix de l'Arc de Triomphe while racing in the stable colors of Godolphin, a collaborative Maktoum family entity.

WINNER'S CIRCLE CHEESE MOLD

FIRST LAYER

8 ounces sharp cheddar cheese, grated

½ cup chopped pecans

¼ cup good-quality mayonnaise

SECOND LAYER

1 (10-ounce) package frozen chopped spinach, drained

1 (8-ounce) package cream cheese, softened

Tabasco sauce to taste

THIRD LAYER

1 (8-ounce) package cream cheese, softened

4 tablespoons chutney

1 teaspoon nutmeg

FOURTH LAYER

8 ounces sharp cheddar cheese, grated

¼ cup chopped pecans

¼ cup good-quality mayonnaise

Parsley for garnish

- Line a 5-inch deep 2-quart mold with plastic wrap using enough to overlap sides of mold.

- In four different batches, separately combine ingredients of each layer in food processor or blender.

- Place first layer firmly and evenly into mold, and follow with remaining layers. Fold plastic wrap over top surface.

- Refrigerate several hours and unmold onto serving plate. Garnish with parsley. Serve with assorted crackers.

SERVES 12 TO 15

SOUR CREAM CORNBREAD

3 eggs, slightly beaten

½ cup vegetable or canola oil

1 cup sour cream

1 small (7-ounce) can cream corn

1 cup self-rising corn meal

- Preheat oven to 450°F.

- Combine eggs and oil. Add sour cream, cream corn, and corn meal one ingredient at a time, blending well after each addition.

- Pour into well-greased 8x8-inch square pan.

- Bake for 20 minutes or until cornbread is golden on top.

SERVES 8

WINTER GREENS

1 tablespoon olive oil

⅓ cup lean bacon, chopped

½ cup onion, finely chopped

1 tablespoon garlic, minced

16 cups greens, Swiss chard, spinach combination, thoroughly washed, stemmed, and chopped

¾ cup chicken stock

24 ounces light ale or beer

1 teaspoon sugar

1½ tablespoons red wine vinegar

1 teaspoon salt

⅛ teaspoon cayenne pepper

¼ teaspoon freshly ground black pepper

- Heat oil in heavy-bottomed, non-reactive pot over medium heat.
- Add bacon and cook for 4 to 5 minutes or until crisp. Remove bacon and reserve.
- Add onion to hot fat and cook, stirring occasionally for 4 minutes or until it starts to soften. Add garlic and cook for 1 minute.
- Return bacon to pot and add greens, stock, ale, sugar, vinegar, and 1 teaspoon of salt.
- Bring greens to a rapid simmer and cook, stirring occasionally, for about 45 minutes, or until thoroughly cooked and tender.
- Season with cayenne pepper, black pepper, and more salt to taste. Serve immediately.

SERVES 4

MARINATED COLE SLAW

¼ cup vegetable oil

½ cup vinegar

½ teaspoon dry mustard

½ cup sugar

¼ teaspoon celery seed

½ teaspoon salt

¼ teaspoon turmeric (optional)

½ large head green cabbage, shredded, or bagged equivalent

¼ large head purple cabbage, shredded, or bagged equivalent

½ large onion, chopped

2 carrots, grated

½ large green bell pepper, chopped

- In saucepan, mix first seven ingredients and bring to boil.
- In large bowl, combine cabbages, onion, carrots, and bell pepper.
- Pour oil and vinegar mixture over cabbages, onion, and bell pepper.
- Marinate and refrigerate for at least 6 hours.

SERVES 5 TO 6

CRISP PARMESAN POTATOES

6 russet potatoes, cut lengthwise into eighths

¼ cup olive oil

½ to 1 teaspoon dried crushed red pepper flakes

½ cup grated Parmesan cheese

Chopped fresh basil for garnish

- Preheat oven to 375°F. Place potatoes on roasting pan.

- Add oil, red pepper, salt, and pepper. Toss potatoes to coat.

- Bake 1 hour, turning once. Season with Parmesan and basil.

SERVES 4

SHADWELL'S VENISON MARINADE

2 pounds venison roast or backstrap

1 cup soy sauce

4 tablespoons olive oil

1 cup water

½ tablespoon Louisiana Hot Sauce (or your favorite hot sauce)

4 tablespoons lemon juice

½ tablespoon black pepper

2 tablespoons brown sugar

1 tablespoon garlic salt

- Combine all marinade ingredients.

- Place venison roast in glass baking dish and pour in marinade. There should be enough volume to reach halfway up the side of roast.

- Place in refrigerator. Turn meat a couple of times a day for two days. The larger the roast, the longer the soaking time.

- Save marinade for basting while cooking.

- Place roast on grill over low heat (250–300°F). Cook slowly; baste with marinade to keep roast juicy.

- Medium (slightly pink on inside) is best for venison. It will get dry if overcooked since there is no marbling in venison.

SERVES 4

OATMEAL CAKE WITH COCONUT PECAN TOPPING

1 cup oatmeal (regular or quick oats)

½ cup unsalted butter

1¼ cups boiling water

1⅓ cups all-purpose flour

1 teaspoon baking soda

½ teaspoon salt

1 teaspoon ground cinnamon

1 teaspoon ground nutmeg

2 eggs

1 cup brown sugar

1 cup granulated sugar

- Preheat oven to 375°F.

- Put oatmeal, butter, and boiling water in bowl and allow to stand for about 20 minutes.

- In another bowl, sift together the flour, baking soda, salt, cinnamon, and nutmeg. Set aside.

- In separate bowl, beat eggs with brown and white sugars. Add to oatmeal mixture. Blend in flour mixture.

- Bake in 9x13-inch baking dish at 375°F for 25 to 30 minutes or until toothpick inserted in cake comes out clean.

SERVES 10 TO 12

COCONUT PECAN TOPPING

½ cup unsalted butter

1 cup brown sugar

¼ cup evaporated milk

1 cup grated coconut

1 cup chopped walnuts or pecans

- Melt butter in saucepan. Add brown sugar, milk, coconut, and nuts.

- Simmer about 10 minutes. Spread on oatmeal cake.

- Place cake under broiler until topping is browned.

SPENDTHRIFT FARM

KENTUCKY WINTER SUPPER

Mini Salmon Croquettes with Parsley Sauce

Fried Chicken

Corn Pudding

Ratatouille

Biscuits

Banana Cake with Caramel Icing

California businessman B. Wayne Hughes purchased Spendthrift Farm in 2004 and set about adding to the glorious traditions of the farm. For some fifty years, when it was headed by Leslie Combs II and then his son, Brownell, Spendthrift was one of the most glamorous of breeding operations. Grand parties were held in the Spendthrift mansion as "Cuzin' Leslie" perfected the art of combining lavish entertainment with the selling of high-priced horses to the same guests. Yearlings by farm stallions became Spendthrift's cash crop, and Keeneland was its marketplace. Combs was the leading consignor by average price for sixteen consecutive years, from 1949 through 1964, at the old Keeneland summer sale. Horses sold include Kentucky Derby–Preakness winner Majestic Prince and filly champion Idun.

Combs also pioneered the age of million-dollar deals when he syndicated the champion Nashua as a stallion prospect for $1,251,250 in 1955. Stallions later to stand at Spendthrift under the Combses' management include Raise a Native and Triple Crown winners Seattle Slew and Affirmed.

Hughes is the sort of self-made businessman that Combs used to love to entertain. Hughes launched Public Storage Inc. with a $50,000 investment in 1972 and made the company the largest owner and operator of self-storage facilities in the United States. Hughes also is active in other real estate investments. He entered racing about 1980 and found Spendthrift's old venue, Keeneland, an attractive recruiting site. Hughes purchased Action This Day at Keeneland, and the colt won the Breeders' Cup Juvenile the next year to become the 2003 champion two-year-old.

MINI SALMON CROQUETTES WITH PARSLEY SAUCE

4 tablespoons butter

1 tablespoon chopped onion

1 tablespoon chopped celery

1 pound cooked salmon or
  1 (14-ounce) can of salmon

1 egg or 2 egg whites

1 cup bread crumbs or panko
  crumbs

2 tablespoons olive oil

Salt and pepper to taste

- Sauté onion and celery in 2 tablespoons butter.

- In a bowl, flake salmon and stir in 1 egg or 2 egg whites. Add onion and celery and mix well. Make 6 small croquettes and roll in dry bread crumbs.

- Allow croquettes to set in refrigerator for at least 2 hours.

- Sauté in olive oil and 2 tablespoons butter until golden brown on each side, about 10 minutes total. Serve with lemon wedges or Parsley Sauce (recipe below).

MAKES 4 TO 6 SMALL CROQUETTES

PARSLEY SAUCE

1 cup skim milk, divided

1 tablespoon cornstarch

2 tablespoons butter

¼ teaspoon black pepper

¾ cup flat-leaf parsley

1½ tablespoons lemon juice

- Combine ¼ cup milk and cornstarch in small saucepan; stir until smooth.

- Add remaining milk, butter, and pepper.

- Cook over medium heat, stirring constantly until mixture comes to a boil. Boil for 1 minute.

- Remove from heat and stir in parsley and lemon juice. Serve as dipping sauce for croquettes.

MAKES APPROXIMATELY 1½ CUPS

FRIED CHICKEN

1 cup all-purpose flour

2 teaspoons salt

1 teaspoon pepper

3 pounds chicken pieces

Approximately 2 cups milk

Shortening

- Combine flour, salt, and pepper in shallow bowl, mixing well. Pour milk into shallow dish. Dip each piece of chicken in milk; then roll in seasoned flour, coating heavily.

- In heavy skillet, melt shortening to ½-inch depth. When shortening is moderately hot, gently lower chicken into it, placing skin side down. Do not crowd pieces; turn and fry until golden brown on all sides.

- Cover skillet and reduce heat; simmer until fork-tender. The meatier pieces will take 25 to 30 minutes; wings and backs will cook more quickly.

- Remove cover last 5 minutes for a crisp crust. Drain chicken on paper towels.

SERVES 4

CORN PUDDING

3 cups fresh corn cut from cob

6 whole eggs, stirred well
   (not beaten)

3 cups heavy cream

1 teaspoon all-purpose flour

½ cup sugar

1 teaspoon salt

½ teaspoon baking powder

2 teaspoons butter, melted

- Preheat oven to 350°F.

- Using a sharp paring knife, barely cut through the tips of the corn kernels to remove from cob; then using the back of the knife blade, scrape the cob to remove the remaining juice and pulp. Place corn in large bowl.

- Stir in eggs and cream.

- Combine dry ingredients and add to corn mixture. Stir in melted butter and mix well.

- Pour into greased baking dish and bake at 350°F for about 1 hour or until knife inserted in center comes out clean.

SERVES 6 TO 8

RATATOUILLE

2 teaspoons olive oil

1 cup chopped onion

3 cups (about 1 pound) fresh
   plum tomatoes, chopped

2 cups chopped, peeled eggplant

1½ cups chopped zucchini

1 cup chopped green bell pepper

1 clove garlic, minced

1 tablespoon chopped
   fresh oregano

1 tablespoon chopped fresh basil

1 tablespoon chopped fresh
   flat-leaf parsley

½ teaspoon salt

¼ teaspoon black pepper

- Heat oil in large skillet over medium-high heat. Add onions and sauté 3 minutes or until tender, stirring frequently.

- Add tomatoes, eggplant, zucchini, bell pepper, and garlic. Cover and reduce heat. Simmer 30 minutes stirring occasionally.

- Stir in oregano and remaining ingredients. Cook, uncovered, 5 minutes or until most of the liquid evaporates.
  (Note: Chopping all the vegetables so that they're the same size will ensure even cooking. This dish is even better 1 or 2 days later. Serve as a side dish, vegetarian entrée with rosemary focaccia, or with sautéed chicken breasts on top. If tomatoes are not in season, you can use a 14.5-ounce can of plum tomatoes.)

SERVES 6 TO 8

BISCUITS

2 cups self-rising flour (or 2 cups
   regular flour and 4 teaspoons
   baking powder)

¾ cup vegetable shortening

¾ cup buttermilk

- Preheat oven to 450°F.

- Cut in shortening to flour with fork. Make a little well and pour in buttermilk all at once. Stir just until moistened (2½ minutes).

- Pour dough onto lightly floured waxed paper. Knead 20 times lightly and pat out to ¾-inch thickness. Cut with biscuit cutter or wine glass but do not twist.

- Place biscuits on greased baking sheet and bake 10 to 12 minutes at 450°F.

MAKES APPROXIMATELY 12 TO 14 BISCUITS

BANANA CAKE WITH CARAMEL ICING

¾ cup unsalted butter

2¼ cups granulated sugar

Juice and grated zest of 1 lemon

3 eggs

1½ cups mashed bananas

3 cups all-purpose flour, sifted

1 teaspoon baking soda

1 teaspoon baking powder

¾ teaspoon salt

⅓ cup buttermilk

- Preheat oven to 350°F.

- Cream butter and sugar. Add lemon juice, zest, and eggs and mix well. Add mashed bananas and mix well.

- In separate bowl, combine dry ingredients. Add flour mixture to banana mixture alternately with buttermilk, stirring until just blended.

- Pour into 3 greased and floured 9x2-inch round layer-cake pans. Bake at 350°F for 25 to 30 minutes. Cool in pans. Then invert the pans to remove cakes onto wire racks to finish cooling.

SERVES 12 TO 14

CARAMEL ICING

1 cup (2 sticks) unsalted butter

10 tablespoons (¾ cup) milk

1 (1-pound) package of light brown sugar

1 teaspoon baking powder

2 teaspoons vanilla

- Place butter, milk, and brown sugar in saucepan. Bring to boil and boil 2 minutes.

- Remove from heat and add baking powder and vanilla. Mix well.

- Frost layers and refrigerate cake.

WALMAC FARM

ASIAN FUSION MEETS THE BLUEGRASS

Shrimp Cakes with Thai Chili Sauce

Asian Stir-Fried Vegetable Salad

Filet Mignon with Shiitake Mushroom Sauce

Green Beans and Cauliflower with Toasted Cashews

Wasabi Mashed Potatoes

Pineapple Lime Sherbet with Ginger Cookies

During the 1940s the name Walmac Farm was associated with the consistent stakes winner Billings. The Walmac of that time was owned by Pure Oil executive R.W. McIlvain. Beginning in the late 1970s, the name Walmac meant the international operation on Paris Pike run by John T.L. Jones Jr. In those days, the farm's fame rested in part on such international stallions as two-time Prix de l'Arc de Triomphe winner Alleged and the versatile sires of classic winners, Nureyev and Miswaki. One of the most remarkable of veterinary success stories was Nureyev's surviving a severe leg fracture in a paddock accident. The farm's dedicated staff and veterinary consultants were instrumental in helping Nureyev through his prolonged struggle.

Walmac over the years also has been prominent as a sponsor of races, including Keeneland's former Walmac Alcibiades Stakes and the Walmac Lone Star Oaks and Walmac Lone Star Derby in Texas.

Since 2005 Walmac Farm has been owned by Jones' son, John T.L. Jones III, in partnership with Robert B. (Bobby) Trussell Jr. The partners operate both Walmac Farm LLC and Walmac Stud Management LLC. Jones' father remains as director emeritus and consultant. The new owners pursued the established emphasis on stallions, and their assumption of control coincided with the burgeoning careers of such young stallions as leading freshman sire Successful Appeal and the speedy Songandaprayer. The stallion division is housed on the main farm of 285 acres, and the Walmac operation also encompasses the 667-acre Bedford Farm Annex. Both offer state-of-the-art facilities for boarding, breeding, and raising and breaking young racehorses.

SHRIMP CAKES WITH THAI CHILI SAUCE

1 pound of uncooked shrimp, peeled, deveined, and coarsely chopped

2 large eggs, lightly beaten

2 scallions, chopped

2 tablespoons fresh lemon juice

½ teaspoon lemon zest

1 tablespoon Dijon mustard

2 tablespoons fresh cilantro, minced

½ teaspoon Thai hot garlic sauce

Dash of salt

Dash of pepper

2 cups panko bread crumbs

4 tablespoons peanut oil

THAI CHILI SAUCE

¼ cup sake

2 limes, zest and juice

1 tablespoon chopped fresh ginger

2 cloves garlic, chopped

2 tablespoons fresh cilantro, chopped

¼ cup heavy cream

2 tablespoons Thai hot garlic sauce

4 tablespoons (½ stick) unsalted butter, chopped into pieces

- In large bowl, mix shrimp, lightly beaten eggs, scallions, lemon juice, lemon zest, mustard, cilantro, Thai hot garlic sauce, salt, and pepper until well blended. Add 1 cup of bread crumbs and mix again.

- Form into small patties and set on parchment-lined baking sheet. Cover with plastic wrap and refrigerate while making sauce.

- Combine sake, lime zest and juice, ginger, garlic, and cilantro in saucepan. Boil on high until reduced by half. Strain liquid through sieve and return to saucepan.

- Add cream and bring back to boil for 2 minutes. Reduce to low. Add Thai hot garlic sauce.

- Whisk butter piece by piece into sauce until well combined. Keep sauce warm while cooking shrimp cakes.

- To cook shrimp cakes, heat 4 tablespoons peanut oil on medium-high in large skillet.

- Press patties in remaining 1 cup of bread crumbs and place in hot oil. Cook patties for 6 minutes, flipping every 2 minutes.

- To serve, drizzle 2 teaspoons of Thai chili sauce in large ring on plate. Place shrimp cake in center and garnish with sprig of cilantro.

YIELDS APPROXIMATELY 6 CAKES

ASIAN STIR-FRIED VEGETABLE SALAD

4 tablespoons peanut oil

2 cups bok choy, chopped

1 small head Napa cabbage, shredded

1 teaspoon red pepper flakes

1 cup frozen edamame, shelled

2 tablespoons tamari

3 scallions, chopped

Sprigs of fresh Thai basil and cilantro

2 tablespoons oyster sauce

1 teaspoon light brown sugar

1 tablespoon sesame oil

2 tablespoons sesame seeds, toasted

- Heat 2 tablespoons of peanut oil in wok or large skillet and cook bok choy, Napa cabbage, and red pepper flakes quickly, until vegetables are just wilted.

- Add edamame, tamari, scallions, basil, and cilantro. Sauté for 1 minute. Transfer to serving plate.

- In small bowl, combine oyster sauce, brown sugar, remaining peanut oil, and sesame oil and pour over greens. Scatter sesame seeds over top and serve immediately.

SERVES 6

FILET MIGNON WITH SHIITAKE MUSHROOM SAUCE

1 whole trimmed filet mignon, at room temperature

1 tablespoon finely minced garlic

2 tablespoons sesame oil

2 teaspoons cracked black pepper, or to taste

1½ teaspoons Celtic sea salt, coarse ground, or to taste

SHIITAKE MUSHROOM SAUCE

¾ cup thinly sliced shiitake mushrooms

2 tablespoons peanut oil

⅔ cup plus 3 tablespoons red wine

1½ teaspoons fresh rosemary, minced

1½ teaspoons fresh thyme, minced

1 bay leaf

3 cups beef stock

2 tablespoons tomato paste

2 tablespoons cornstarch

- Preheat oven to 425°F.

- Sear whole tenderloin filet on hot grill for about 5 minutes total.

- In small bowl, combine garlic, oil, pepper, and salt. Rub mixture onto seared meat and arrange meat on rack in roasting pan. Roast meat for 30 minutes, or until meat thermometer inserted in thickest part of tenderloin registers 130°F to 140°F for medium-rare.

- Once done, transfer meat to cutting board and let rest, loosely covered with foil, for 10 minutes.

- In very hot skillet, add peanut oil and shiitake mushrooms and sauté about 3 minutes.

- Transfer mushrooms to saucepan and add ⅔ cup wine, rosemary, thyme, and bay leaf, and simmer until reduced about ⅓. Add beef stock and tomato paste. Simmer for 15 minutes.

- In small bowl, combine remaining wine with cornstarch until smooth. Blend into sauce. Simmer for 5 more minutes, or until sauce is lightly thickened. Remove bay leaf before serving.

SERVES 6 TO 8

GREEN BEANS AND CAULIFLOWER WITH TOASTED CASHEWS

1 small head of cauliflower, cut into florets

½ pound green beans, ends trimmed

2 tablespoons peanut oil

1 tablespoon chili oil

1 small onion, chopped

2 cloves garlic, chopped

1 teaspoon Thai red curry paste

½ cup low sodium vegetable bouillon

2 tablespoons tamari

1 tablespoon hoisin sauce

½ cup toasted cashews, to garnish

- Parboil cauliflower and green beans until crisp-tender.

- Heat both oils in wok or large skillet and stir-fry onion and garlic until softened. Add curry paste and stir-fry for 1 to 2 minutes.

- Add parboiled cauliflower and green beans and stir-fry for 2 minutes. Pour in bouillon, tamari, and hoisin sauce and simmer for 1 to 2 minutes. Serve immediately, garnished with cashews.

SERVES 6

WASABI MASHED POTATOES

2 pounds russet potatoes, peeled and quartered

4 tablespoons (½ stick) unsalted butter, at room temperature

1 cup half & half, warmed

Freshly ground black pepper to taste

1 teaspoon wasabi or to taste

1 tablespoon scallions, chopped

- Place potatoes in large pot with cold water to cover by about 1 inch. Bring to boil over high heat, reduce heat to medium-low, and simmer until potatoes are just tender. Drain potatoes.

- Use potato ricer to mash potatoes. Stir in butter, half & half, black pepper, and wasabi until combined. Top with chopped scallions. Serve immediately.

SERVES 6 TO 8

PINEAPPLE LIME SHERBET

1 cup superfine sugar

2½ cups water

Grated zest and juice of 2 limes

1 small pineapple, peeled, cored, quartered, and chopped

- Put sugar and water into pan and heat gently, stirring, until sugar has dissolved. Bring to boil and simmer for 10 minutes to form syrup. Stir in grated zest and half the lime juice. Remove from heat and let cool.

- Place pineapple in blender or food processor and process until smooth. Add to cold syrup with remaining lime juice.

- Pour into freezer-proof container and freeze until crystals have formed around edge of pineapple mixture.

- Remove sherbet from freezer and transfer to bowl. Beat well with fork to break up any ice crystals. Return to freezer in freezer-proof container and chill overnight.

- Serve in scoops with thin, crisp ginger cookies (recipe below).

SERVES 6

GINGER COOKIES

¾ cup margarine

1 cup sugar

¼ cup molasses

1 egg

2 cups all-purpose flour

¼ teaspoon salt

2 teaspoons baking soda

1 teaspoon cloves

1 teaspoon cinnamon

1 teaspoon ground ginger

- Cream margarine and sugar with electric mixer. Add molasses and egg. Beat well.

- Sift all dry ingredients together and add to egg mixture, beating until well incorporated.

- Refrigerate until chilled or overnight.

- Preheat oven to 325°F.

- Roll cookie dough into small balls. Roll balls in granulated sugar and place on cookie sheet 2 inches apart as cookies will spread as they bake. Flatten balls with bottom of a glass.

- Bake at 325°F for 15 minutes. Allow cookies to cool slightly on sheet and then transfer to wax paper to cool completely.

MAKES APPROXIMATELY 3 DOZEN SMALL COOKIES

XALAPA FARM

WINTER BRUNCH

Milk Punch

Endive and Granny Smith Apple Salad

Grillades and Grits

Eggs Benedict

Garlic Bread

Homemade Peppermint Ice Cream

Once the dream of a proud Kentuckian, Xalapa Farm near Paris has been maintained as an enclosed enclave where horses roam lush fields while woods of oak, sycamore, and walnut shade lovely gardens and the main residence. Edward F. Simms founded Xalapa in 1897 after venturing from his native state to study at Yale and the University of Virginia and later finding success in the oilfields of Texas and Louisiana. Simms established an important breeding operation, and his importation of Prince Palatine brought to Xalapa what would prove an ancestor in the bloodlines of milestone horses such as Northern Dancer, Mr. Prospector, Native Dancer, and Alydar.

Simms' great-granddaughter, Celeste, and her husband, Emler Neuman, preserve the quiet elegance of Xalapa today while also operating a thriving business of raising, prepping, and rehabbing clients' Thoroughbreds. Facilities have been expanded and include a newly renovated stone crescent barn and a new foaling barn. Although modern, the foaling barn was built of sturdy logs to blend with the history felt everywhere at Xalapa. The family's breeding operation in recent years has added to the farm's legacy, producing horses such as Prix de l'Arc de Triomphe winner Suave Dancer.

MILK PUNCH

1 gallon whole milk (or half milk, half cream)

6 cups Kentucky bourbon

1 cup powdered sugar

2 tablespoons vanilla

Freshly ground nutmeg

- Thoroughly mix gallon of milk with bourbon, powdered sugar, and vanilla.

- Pour over ice and top with freshly ground nutmeg.

SERVES 8

ENDIVE AND GRANNY SMITH APPLE SALAD

10 heads of endive

3 Granny Smith apples

½ pound walnuts

- Finely chop endive and dice Granny Smith apples. Mix and lightly coat mixture with mustard dressing (recipe below).

- Toast walnuts at 350°F for approximately 8 minutes, then place atop salad.

SERVES 8

MUSTARD DRESSING

¼ cup Zatarain's Creole Mustard

3 tablespoons light brown sugar

¼ cup light olive oil

Salt and pepper to taste

Orange juice

- Blend mustard and brown sugar. Slowly add olive oil to thicken.

- Salt and pepper to taste. If too thick, add orange juice. Drizzle over endive and Granny Smith apple salad.

GRILLADES

4 pounds veal or beef rounds,
½-inch thick

½ cup bacon drippings

½ cup all-purpose flour

1 cup chopped onion

2 cups chopped scallions

¾ cup chopped celery

1½ cups chopped
green bell peppers

2 cloves garlic, minced

2½ cups chopped tomatoes

⅔ teaspoon thyme

1 cup water

1 cup red wine

3 teaspoons salt

½ teaspoon black pepper

2 bay leaves

¾ teaspoon Tabasco sauce

2 tablespoons
Worcestershire sauce

3 tablespoons chopped
flat-leaf parsley

- Remove fat from meat and pound to ¼-inch thickness. Cut meat into serving-size pieces, approximately 2-inch squares.

- In Dutch oven, brown meat well in batches in 4 tablespoons of bacon grease. Remove browned meat to warm plate.

- To Dutch oven, add 4 more tablespoons bacon grease and flour. Stir and cook to make dark brown roux. Be careful not to burn roux.

- Add onions, scallions, celery, green bell pepper, garlic, and cook until vegetables are limp.

- Add tomatoes and thyme, and cook for 3 minutes. Add water and wine. Stir well for several minutes; then return meat to mixture.

- Add salt, black pepper, bay leaves, and Tabasco and Worcestershire sauces. Lower heat, stir, and continue cooking, covered, for approximately 1 hour.

- Remove bay leaves. Stir in parsley and cool.

- Let grillades sit several hours or overnight in refrigerator.

- When ready to serve, reheat grillades, adding more liquid if needed.

- Serve over grits or rice.

SERVES 6 TO 8

EGGS BENEDICT

8 Holland rusks or English muffins

8 slices Canadian bacon, grilled

8 soft poached eggs

- Cover Holland rusks or English muffins with grilled Canadian bacon.
- Top with eggs.
- Spoon hollandaise sauce (recipe below) over eggs. Serve immediately.

SERVES 8

HOLLANDAISE SAUCE

4 egg yolks

2 tablespoons lemon juice

½ pound unsalted butter, chilled and cut into 2-inch slices

¼ teaspoon salt

- In top half of double boiler or in heavy-bottomed pot, beat egg yolks and stir in lemon juice.
- Whisking continuously, gradually add butter, one piece at a time, until incorporated.
- Keep whisking and do not let sauce come to a boil. When thickened, add salt and remove from heat. Sauce will "keep" over low heat for about 1 hour.

GARLIC BREAD

½ cup (1 stick) butter, softened

2 tablespoons minced garlic

¼ cup Parmesan cheese

Salt and pepper to taste

½ teaspoon dried thyme

1 loaf quality French bread
or baguette

- Preheat oven to 425°F. In a small bowl, combine butter, garlic, cheese, salt, pepper, and thyme to form a paste.

- Place whole loaf of bread into a heated oven until very lightly browned on the outside, about 8 minutes. Remove from oven.

- Slice bread lengthwise and place halved sections on baking sheet, cut side up.

- Generously spread butter-garlic spread on sliced halves.

- Return to oven under broiler. Broil until golden and bubbly. Watch to avoid burning.

- Slice halves into smaller pieces for serving.

SERVES 8

HOMEMADE PEPPERMINT ICE CREAM

3 cups heavy cream

1 cup whole milk

½ cup plus 2 tablespoons sugar

4 egg yolks

2 cups crushed peppermint sticks

4 drops peppermint oil

- Heat cream, milk, and sugar in heavy-bottomed saucepan, stirring until sugar is dissolved and mixture is hot.

- Place egg yolks in medium bowl and whisk. While whisking, slowly pour in about a cup of the hot liquid. Gradually incorporate milk mixture with beaten eggs until mixture thickens and coats back of spoon.

- While mixture is warm, add 2 cups of crushed peppermint sticks and 4 drops of peppermint oil. Mix well.

- Refrigerate until cooled and pour into ice cream maker and freeze according to directions on your machine.

MAKES APPROXIMATELY 1 PINT

INDEX

ACKNOWLEDGMENTS

The Garden Club of Lexington wishes to thank the farms that contributed to *Entertaining With Bluegrass Winners* and the photographers who captured the beauty of Bluegrass horse country, including:

Anne M. Eberhardt
Joy Gilbert
Dell Hancock
Dan Dry
Marthea Kelley
Barbara D. Livingston
Andrew de Lory
Michael J. Marten
David Middleton
John Nation
Suzie Picou Oldham
Doug Prather
Kirk Schlea
Amy Sword
Lee Thomas